PRAISE FOR *TRUTH AND REPAIR*

"Through masterful storytelling, Judith Herman charts the course from trauma to justice and compels us to follow it. An inspiring and practical call to action, *Truth and Repair* celebrates survivors' wisdom and their power to heal themselves and the world we live in."

—Anita Hill

"Three decades after the publication of her foundational *Trauma and Recovery*, Herman brilliantly confronts us with another vital, but much ignored, aspect of recovery: social justice. Justice is an essential component for healing the godforsaken sense of humiliation and abandonment so central in traumatizing experiences. When justice is denied, trauma's imprint is likely to fester in the form of helpless rage. A magnificent and inspiring contribution with profound implications for the healing professions and for society at large."

—Bessel van der Kolk, MD, author of the #1 *New York Times* bestseller *The Body Keeps the Score*

"Herman has written some of the most seminal, life-changing books on violence against women. Here in her new book, *Truth and Repair*, she does something even more radical. She listens to the survivors themselves and skillfully shapes their voices and wisdom into a practical and truly enlightened road map for our future. Every word rang true and essential."

—V (formerly Eve Ensler), playwright of *The Vagina Monologues*

"For thirty years, every single book written about the impact of trauma has stood on the shoulders of Herman's groundbreaking book *Trauma and Recovery*. Now, thirty years later, we receive a bookend to that masterpiece, examining how survivors of gender-based violence seek justice and healing. *Truth and Repair* is a deeply researched and thought-provoking book offering hope and healing for victims of violence, many of whom have felt betrayed, ignored, or retraumatized by existing larger societal institutions."

—Michelle Bowdler, author of *Is Rape a Crime?*

"Herman's earlier studies of abuse of women and children recast our understanding of trauma. Now, in *Truth and Repair*, she comes full circle in describing how initially powerless victims can, through innovative social arrangements, achieve hard-won survivor justice. In the process, we learn much about what justice really means for traumatized people. Herman's perspective is deeply humane and grounded in historical and political reality. Her work stands alone in its arc and originality."

—Robert Jay Lifton, MD, Columbia University

Also by Judith L. Herman

Father-Daughter Incest

Trauma and Recovery: The Aftermath of Violence—
from Domestic Abuse to Political Terror

TRUTH AND REPAIR

HOW TRAUMA SURVIVORS ENVISION JUSTICE

JUDITH L. HERMAN, MD

BASIC BOOKS

New York

Basic Books

Hachette Book Group

1290 Avenue of the Americas, New York, NY 10104

www.basicbooks.com

Printed in the United States of America

First Edition: March 2023

Published by Basic Books, an imprint of Perseus Books, LLC, a subsidiary of Hachette Book Group, Inc. The Basic Books name and logo is a trademark of the Hachette Book Group.

The Hachette Speakers Bureau provides a wide range of authors for speaking events. To find out more, go to www.hachettespeakersbureau.com or call (866) 376-6591.

The publisher is not responsible for websites (or their content) that are not owned by the publisher.

Print book interior design by Amy Quinn.

Library of Congress Cataloging-in-Publication Data

Names: Herman, Judith Lewis, 1942- author.

Title: Truth and repair : how trauma survivors envision justice / Judith L. Herman, MD.

Description: First edition. | New York : Basic Books, 2023. | Includes bibliographical references and index.

Identifiers: LCCN 2022046067 | ISBN 9781541600546 (hardcover) | ISBN 9781541600560 (ebook)

Subjects: LCSH: Sexual abuse victims--Psychology. | Victims of family violence--Psychology.

Classification: LCC HV6625 .H47 2023 | DDC 362.883--dc23/eng/20221108

LC record available at https://lccn.loc.gov/2022046067

ISBNs: 9781541600546 (hardcover), 9781541600560 (ebook)

LSC-C

Printing 1, 2022

CONTENTS

INTRODUCTION

When I first wrote the forgotten history of trauma, in *Trauma and Recovery*, I argued that the suffering of traumatized people is a matter not only of individual psychology but also, always, of social justice. Because the violence at the source of trauma aims at domination and oppression, even to recognize trauma, to name it, requires the historical context of broad social movements for human rights: for secular democracy, for the abolition of slavery, for women's liberation, for an end to war. Posttraumatic stress disorder was recognized as a legitimate diagnosis in the United States only after Vietnam veterans threw their medals over the White House fence and testified that, even safely returned home, in their minds they were forever in Vietnam. Sexual violence was recognized as a worldwide plague only after women found their voices in the women's liberation movement and testified to the hidden everyday crimes of rape, battery, and incest.

If traumatic disorders are afflictions of the powerless, then empowerment must be a central principle of recovery. If trauma shames and isolates, then recovery must take place in community. These are the central therapeutic insights of my work, and I believe they have held up well across cultures and over time.

In *Trauma and Recovery*, I traced the course of recovery from trauma roughly in three stages. In the first stage, the survivor must focus on the complex and demanding task of establishing safety in the present, with the goal of protection from further violence. Safety allows the survivor to recover from the terror that reduced her to abject submission and to regain a sense of agency. A sense of having some control and choice in daily life is in turn a prerequisite for further recovery. This is why even well-intentioned interventions by police and agents of the justice system can cause further harm when they take power and control away from the survivor and why legal interventions that respect and empower survivors are a just and healing way to make amends for the harms they have suffered.

In the second stage of recovery, the survivor can revisit the past in order to grieve and make meaning of the trauma. She will never be the same person she was before the traumatic events in her life, but out of her grief she can forge a new identity that neither denies her past nor allows it to define her entirely. Tracing the recovery of survivors over time, a large body of research has now documented facts that make intuitive sense: social support is a powerful predictor of good recovery, while social isolation is toxic. People cannot feel safe alone, and they cannot mourn and make meaning alone.

Mourning the past may seem endless, but it does come to an end. In the third stage, the survivor can refocus on the present and future, expanding and deepening her relationships with a wider community and her sense of possibility in life.[1] Some extraordinary survivors, recognizing that their suffering is part of a much larger social problem, are able to transform the meaning of their trauma by making their stories a gift to others and by joining with others to seek a better world. They develop what my colleague and friend Robert Jay Lifton has called a "survivor mission."[2] Over the years, it has been my privilege to be a witness and ally of the many patients who have passed through these stages of recovery to reclaim their lives.

In recent years, I have begun to contemplate the idea of a fourth and final stage of recovery, and that is justice. If trauma is truly a social problem, and indeed it is, then recovery cannot be simply a private, individual matter. The wounds of trauma are not merely those caused by the perpetrators of violence and exploitation; the actions or inactions of bystanders—all those who are complicit in or who prefer not to know about the abuse or who blame the victims—often cause even deeper wounds. These wounds are part of the social ecology of violence, in which crimes against subordinated and marginalized people are rationalized, tolerated, or rendered invisible. If trauma originates in a fundamental injustice, then full healing must require repair through some measure of justice from the larger community.

In the course of their recovery, survivors inevitably confront many complicated questions about justice: Can they dare to tell their stories in public, and if so, can their truth be recognized by the community? Can the harm be repaired, and if so, what would that require? How can survivors and offenders go on living in the same community? What would it mean to hold offenders accountable? Is reconciliation something to be desired, and if so, how can it be achieved? How can the community provide public safety and prevent future harm?

To try to answer these questions, I have, once more, listened to survivors. This book is about envisioning a better way of justice for all. I propose that survivors of violence, who know in their bones the truths that many others would prefer not to know, can lead the way to a new understanding of justice. The first step is simply to ask survivors what would make things right—or as right as possible—for them. This sounds like such a reasonable thing to do, but in practice, it is hardly ever done. Listening, therefore, turns out to be a radical act.

In this book I try to show what justice means to many survivors—and, through their ideas, to envision how very different our justice systems might be if their needs and wishes were truly taken into account. I have focused in particular on survivors of violence against women and children for two reasons: (1) because we now know that this may be the most prevalent and enduring human rights violation in the world,[3] and (2) because these survivors are the people whom I have worked with the most throughout my professional career.

I came of age during the women's liberation movement, which taught me the radical act of listening. This was my great good fortune. As the author Grace Paley has written, women who took part in the movement in those years were supported by "the buoyancy, the noise, the saltiness" of that great Second Wave,[4] and indeed, I have relied on that support ever since. A few months before I began my psychiatric residency, in 1970, I joined a consciousness-raising group. My friend and college classmate Kathie Sarachild, who had been a civil rights worker in the Deep South, had seen there the power of people gathering to tell their own stories. She named consciousness raising as a method of both political organizing and scientific inquiry. In a book of essays called *Feminist Revolution*, published by a group called New York Redstockings, Kathie wrote, "We would be the first to dare to do and say the undareable, what women really felt and wanted."[5]

The confidential space of the psychotherapy office had many similarities with the free space of the women's movement, and as my patients revealed their secrets, I listened with a new awareness of women's condition. My first two patients on the inpatient service where I began my training were women who had made serious suicide attempts. Both disclosed histories of father-daughter incest. It was not hard to see the connection between their despair and their early initiation into the life of a sexual object. I wrote in my journal, "In patriarchy the father maintains the right to sex with his daughter in the same way that the feudal lord maintains the *jus primae noctis* with his subjects." Incest seemed to me like a paradigm of women's sexual oppression.

After completing my residency, I went to work in a women's free storefront clinic in Somerville, Massachusetts, a city on the outskirts of Boston that was then a bastion of the mostly Irish American white working class. The clinic was one of the many "counter-institutions," like rape crisis centers and battered women's shelters, that activists in the women's movement created during the early 1970s. There I saw more women with incest histories. I began to investigate this further, in collaboration with my friend and colleague Lisa Hirschman, who had just received her doctorate in psychology. Within a short time we had collected twenty cases just by asking a few other therapists we knew. At that time, a major psychiatry textbook estimated the prevalence of incest as one case per million.[6] These eminent authorities were wrong by four orders of magnitude, willfully blinded to the widespread prevalence of child abuse. We would never have dared to contradict these authorities alone, but with the energy and passion of the women's movement behind us, and with the honor of having been entrusted with our patients' secrets, we could become public witnesses to the reality of women's condition. We decided to publish our findings.

In 1975, Lisa and I submitted our paper to a new women's studies journal.[7] A year elapsed between the paper's acceptance and its publication. During that year, the paper was copied and passed from hand to hand, like samizdat, and soon we started getting letters from women all over the country, saying, "I thought I was the only one," or "I thought no one would believe me," or "I thought it was my fault." By listening to women and daring to publish what we found, we had become catalysts for a transformative moment, when crimes long hidden were revealed. As clinicians, we were also privileged to witness the liberation that comes when the burdens of shame and fear are lifted. As our patients told their stories and were met with compassion rather than scorn, their despair gave way to renewed hope, and their isolation to a renewed sense of community.

In 1981 I published my first book, *Father-Daughter Incest*, elaborating upon the significance of these discoveries. It followed a train of books published in the 1970s by Second Wave feminists that laid bare the dimensions of violence against women.[8] My work, throughout my professional career, has been built on those initial revelations of that revolutionary moment.[9]

In that same year, I was invited to join the psychiatry department of Cambridge Hospital, a public "safety-net" hospital that served the poor and marginalized. It had recently become a teaching hospital for Harvard Medical School, and at the time this new psychiatry department had the energy and creativity of a start-up. The faculty members were interested in developing community models of psychiatric care and were making original contributions to the field. Though the leadership group was all male, they were willing to include a couple of females who seemed to have some moxie. This was surely the only place within the Harvard ecosystem where I could have found the freedom to bring the knowledge and wisdom gained in the women's movement into the largely clueless world of academic psychiatry.

My colleague Mary Harvey, a community psychologist who had studied exemplary rape crisis programs at the National Institute of Mental Health, and I began with a small grant from the City of Cambridge to develop mental health services for crime victims. Over time, we built this into the Victims of Violence (VoV) Program, a center that provided clinical care and advocacy for patients, training in trauma treatment for mental health professionals, and crisis response following incidents of violence that affected whole communities.

At the VoV Program, once again many of our patients were women (and some men) burdened with the enduring consequences of childhood abuse and sexual and domestic violence. We also saw refugees who were seeking asylum from political persecution. During the early 1980s, I also took part in a trauma study group, organized by my friend Bessel van der Kolk, that brought together clinicians and researchers working with combat veterans, abused children, and survivors of rape and domestic violence. It became clear to me that just as oppression is oppression, trauma is trauma, whether in the public domain of war and politics or the supposedly private domain of sex, reproduction, and family life. On the basis of these insights, I wrote *Trauma and Recovery*, published in 1992.

The VoV Program has now trained some two hundred psychiatrists, psychologists, and social workers; many have gone on to make their own original contributions to the trauma field. Over the years we have witnessed the dialectic of trauma unfolding, times when advances in understanding were powered by the alliances between the survivors who told their stories and the professionals who bore witness, followed by times of social backlash and professional constriction. Now, with the inspiration of a new wave of worldwide consciousness-raising movements proclaiming the truth of women's lives, Black lives, and the lived experiences of those who have been dishonored and scorned, I have returned to talk once more with the kind of trauma survivors whose testimony has shaped my intellectual and professional life.

In what follows, I draw on work in philosophy, social science, history, law, and psychology and on interviews with professionals who work directly with survivors as attorneys, judges, advocates, educators, and, of course, mental health professionals. But at its heart my book is based on the testimony of survivors themselves, for I argue that they are the experts on what some have begun to call survivors' justice or healing justice. Emboldened by the grassroots freedom movements, an increasing number of survivors have published their own first-person accounts. In addition, I have conducted unstructured, in-depth interviews with many survivors from diverse backgrounds who heard about my project through my various professional social networks and who were willing to talk with me. These remarkable women and men are people with a survivor mission: they have been able to create new purpose in life from their trauma by sharing their stories. Some have devoted their lives to efforts to prevent violence, as teachers, writers, artists, attorneys, community organizers, clergy, and victim advocates. Some were willing to be identified by name; others chose pseudonyms for this purpose. I quote from their interviews throughout the book.

One of the survivors who spoke with me is a young woman named Sarah Super, a community organizer living in Minneapolis. Her story illustrates both the best that the conventional justice system offers and a vision of justice that goes far beyond it. Sarah first got in touch with me a few years ago to invite me to a groundbreaking ceremony for a memorial for sexual assault survivors. She had read *Trauma and Recovery* and was inspired by a chapter in which I compared rape and combat as violent initiation rites for young men and women. I wrote about the importance of the Vietnam War Memorial in Washington, DC, as a place of public recognition, pilgrimage, and healing for

Vietnam veterans and contrasted this with the fact that there was no memorial anywhere for rape victims. Sarah decided that she wanted to get her city to build one. And she did.

Sarah had endured a terrifying assault by an ex-boyfriend, who broke into her apartment at night and raped her at knifepoint. Afterward, she managed to flee, screamed, and was taken in by neighbors. In this rare instance, the justice system functioned exactly the way it is supposed to do. "The police were there within minutes," she said. "I was treated really well. I lived on a beautiful street, very white, very affluent. I was the perfect victim." Alec, the rapist, fled and was arrested after a highway chase. "He was also treated really well," Sarah reflected. "I often thought of how they took him into custody without harm." She wondered what would have happened to him if he were Black.

Alec eventually pled guilty and was sentenced to twelve years in prison. Sarah felt that the severity of the sentence validated the severity of the crime because he had threatened her life and also because she believed he was still dangerous and she was still afraid of him: "He may want to punish me for holding him accountable," she said, "since he punished me for breaking up with him." She felt well supported by her victim advocate and the district attorney who prosecuted her case, and at the sentencing, she had a chance to tell her story, and she felt heard: "When I read my victim impact statement," Sarah reported, "[the judge] took her glasses off and really listened."

What, then, was missing? What else was needed for justice to be done? For Sarah, one of the most hurtful parts of the whole experience was the way that the rape divided the supposedly liberal community to which both she and Alec belonged.

His parents, who had often welcomed her into their home, apparently considered themselves and Alec to be the real victims since he was facing criminal charges, and they started a "Care Hub" to organize community support for him, including money for his defense and a letter-writing campaign testifying to his "good character." Meantime, Sarah heard nothing from them. She felt erased. A few weeks after the rape, Sarah chose to identify herself in the Minneapolis press as the victim of his crime. She was hurt once again by how few people she knew said anything to her in response. "I felt the silence that surrounds sexual violence," she said. "I saw how that silence isolates survivors, protects perpetrators, and allows for the community to support rape culture as ignorant, passive bystanders."

This is what happens with crimes of sexual violence. They divide communities as they lay bare the underlying power dynamics of dominance and subordination. In the aftermath of the rape, Sarah said, everyday sexism became intolerable to her. But when she began dating again, she could see how deeply ingrained it was in the culture. She talked with the men she dated about their sexual attitudes and experiences. All of them had been to bachelor parties at strip clubs and had used pornography as a regular part of their lives. She was the first person who ever asked them about some of the ways they participated in rape culture, she said. They had never thought about it before. They didn't see any need to think about it. "Justice involves cultural change," she said. "Healing would depend on a world where initiation rites for young men don't involve degrading women."

Though Sarah had not heard from many friends and colleagues whom she had expected to be supportive, she had heard from many, many strangers who shared their stories. "I learned I had been surrounded by survivors of sexual violence without knowing it," she said. This is ultimately what made her determined to create a memorial where the reality of sexual violence could be publicly recognized. Sarah recounts, "I wrote to my city council member (for the first time ever), who pointed me to my Park Board Commissioner (whom I didn't know), who invited me to speak for three minutes during an upcoming Park Board Meeting."

As a skillful organizer, Sarah invited the many survivors who had written to her to join her as she read her three-minute statement to the Park Board. As a result of her leadership and the outpouring of stories that occurred at a moment of societal reckoning about sexual abuses of power, the Memorial to Survivors of Sexual Violence has now been built in a Minneapolis park. It was dedicated on October 10, 2020. Tarana Burke, the Black community organizer who founded the #MeToo movement, and V (formerly known as Eve Ensler), the white playwright who wrote *The Vagina Monologues*, spoke at the dedication. Sarah envisions the monument as a place for public education and "community truth-telling" events. One of the mosaics from the memorial, by the artist Lori Greene, illustrates the cover of this book.

Honoring survivors with public recognition is a kind of justice very different from conventional notions of what justice means. But this kind of recognition means a great deal to survivors, as it helps to heal their broken relationship with their communities—which I argue is essential to survivors' justice. As we've learned most recently from the bitter reckoning with our country's numerous monuments to the Confederacy, memorials do matter. They are enduring public proclamations that tell us whom our society honors and respects. Sometimes directly, more often by omission, they also tell us who is to be dishonored and disrespected, who is to be invisible.

Many monuments to the Confederacy were established after the Civil War, during the period of reaction that instituted a century of lynch law and Jim Crow. It was a profound moment, therefore, when the National Memorial for Peace and Justice, founded by Black attorney Bryan Stevenson and the Equal Justice Initiative, was dedicated in Montgomery, Alabama, in 2018. Informally known as the National Lynching Memorial, it honors four thousand victims of white supremacist atrocities by name, and it challenges each of the communities where they were murdered to acknowledge its own unspoken history. In the same way, a monument to victims of sexual assault is a public vindication of survivors that challenges the unspoken entitlements of male supremacy. The public recognition of hidden wrongs in many ways represents a first step toward equal justice.

Sarah Super's story illustrates the kind of public affirmation for survivors that is lacking even in the best of what the conventional justice system has to offer. But in reality, the great majority of survivors never find justice, even in conventional terms. Sarah was treated with respect and professionalism by police officers, a prosecutor, and a judge. Most sexual assault survivors never encounter any of these public servants, or if they do, they dearly wish they had not. Police often interrogate them as though they were suspects rather than victims. Prosecutors don't want to be bothered with cases that might be difficult to win because of common prejudices that juries might share. Judges often share these prejudices as well. Survivors who have had encounters with the justice system often speak of them as a "second rape." Members of other subordinated or marginalized groups suffer similar injustices. As we have learned from the movement for Black lives, police violence against people of color, up to and including murder, is basically a crime of impunity. It is time that we seek something better.

The book is divided into three parts. Part One lays out the underlying theory that justice depends on the social organization of power. In Chapters 1 and 2, I contrast two fundamentally different types of power relationship, one based on dominance and subordination and the other based on mutuality and reciprocity. The first is the archetype of tyranny; the second, the archetype of equality. Both types of power relationship are found worldwide and throughout history, and both are found on every scale of human interaction and social structure, from the intimate realms of love and family, to the political realms of the nation-state, to the international realms of organized religion, business, and crime. The first is found in histories of war, conquest, enslavement, and genocide; the second is found in the evolution of human attachment and care and in the histories of human aspirations for liberty, peace, and justice. I develop the idea that justice is a moral concept that requires a moral community for its enactment, and I argue that relationships of dominance and subordination are incompatible with justice, which must be based on principles of trust and fairness that are found only in relationships of mutuality.

In Chapter 3, I explore the worldwide hegemony of patriarchy as an example of how the rules and methods of tyranny can be deeply embedded in the organization of social relationships. I detail some of the ways that the hidden violence of patriarchy is perpetuated not only in culture and custom but also in the structures of law, law enforcement, and justice itself. I use the example of patriarchy because this is the example I know best, both personally and professionally. By extension, I hope this analysis can be applied to other situations where the dominance of one group over another is deeply embedded over centuries, as in the legacies of caste, slavery, colonialism, and religious persecution. For the same reasons, most of the research and testimony I cite comes from the United States; by extension I hope similar methods of analysis can be extended to other countries.

Part Two elaborates the visions of justice that emerge from the testimonies of my informants. I outline the fundamental contrast between what so many survivors say they want, which is truth and repair, and what our justice system actually provides, which is punishment and monetary damages. Chapter 4 is about public acknowledgment of the truth as the necessary beginning of justice. Every survivor I interviewed for this book, and I daresay every survivor with whom I have ever worked, has wished above all for acknowledgment and vindication. Survivors want the truth to be recognized and the crime to be denounced by those in their communities who matter to them. But this means that survivors must actually matter to their wider communities. It also means that their credibility must be judged without prejudice.

When members of subordinated groups come forward to seek justice, it quickly becomes clear just how little they do matter and how little credit is given to their testimony. For example, after the popular entertainer R. Kelly was recently found guilty of sex trafficking and racketeering, distinguished law professor Kimberlé Crenshaw observed that this famous predator had been able to get away with abusing numerous victims over decades "for the simple reason that people in the overlapping worlds of entertainment, law, and media have been trained to see Black girls and women as dispensable." She added, "If the interplay of racism and misogyny that facilitates the abuse of Black women and girls continues to be taken for granted as background noise, the opportunity to correct the wider historical wrongs that this shameful saga represents will pass."[10] Justice requires not only the criminal conviction of one particularly notorious predator but also, and especially, the correction of those wider historical wrongs.

In Chapters 5 and 6, I elaborate on a vision of justice that centers on repairing the harm to survivors and correcting wider historical wrongs rather than on punishing perpetrators. After acknowledgment of the harm that has been done, the first step toward repairing a damaged relationship is apology. This is the subject of Chapter 5. Here I contrast genuine and insincere apologies. Genuine apologies, though rare, can be extraordinarily healing, while insincere apologies compound the harm. Genuine apologies can often lead to forgiveness and reconciliation, but I argue that social pressure for forgiveness can also become an easy path for bystanders and a trap that compounds injustice for survivors. Chapter 6 explores visions of what accountability for offenders might look like if punishment were not the metric of justice. I review the alternative theories and practices of the restorative justice movement, considering both its creative promise and its limitations. I also review some recent efforts within existing civil law to hold accountable institutions that have enabled widespread criminal exploitation of women and children.

Part Three develops further the idea of justice as healing for victims, perpetrators, and the larger society. Chapter 7 explores the issue of restitution for survivors, beginning with the existing concepts of monetary damages for individuals but expanding the frame to consider the kinds of community organization that will be needed to create truly reparative services within the practices of law and law enforcement.

The last two chapters try to imagine how to prevent future harm. If punishment and sequestration of offenders is not to be the metric of justice, then other ways must be found to provide for community safety and to reintegrate offenders into their communities. Chapter 8 reviews what little is known about offenders and offender rehabilitation. I consider the evidence for the effectiveness of offender treatment, which at present is mainly limited to that small minority who have run afoul of the law and been mandated to treatment by the courts. I also underscore the difference between treatments that are based on the understanding of these crimes as abuses of power and those that lack any underlying social theory. Finally, in Chapter 9, I consider the promise of the college campus as a laboratory for developing new models for preventing gender-based violence, using the frames of both public health and social justice. The book concludes with a visionary Survivors' Agenda.

Listening to trauma survivors and bearing witness to their stories has been the foundation of my professional life for the past fifty years. But this book has also caused me to wander into realms of knowledge and thought, in law and history and political philosophy, far from my own areas of expertise. Think of this book, then, as a beginner's attempt to reimagine justice, based on the testimony of survivors. It will be for others in the future, if indeed our flawed human species has a future on this earth, to build on these ideas.

A NOTE ABOUT
METHODOLOGY

The testimonies I have gathered came from twenty-six women and four men who are survivors of childhood sexual abuse, sexual assault, sex trafficking, sexual harassment, and/or domestic violence. To find them, I simply put out the word through my various professional networks that I was seeking to talk with survivors about their views of justice. I make no pretense that this group is representative of survivors in general. The group I recruited was quite diverse in terms of ethnicity, sexual orientation, and class and geographic background, but on average they were more highly educated than the general population, with many, like myself, in academia or in the professions. They ranged in age from twenty-two to sixty, with most people in their thirties or forties. I did not interview anyone who had been a patient at the Victims of Violence Program. (That would constitute a violation of professional boundaries.) I also did not interview anyone under twenty-one or anyone who was in crisis after a recent assault; all my informants had had some time to recover and reflect on what justice might mean to them.

My group of informants was atypical, also, in that over half had reported the crimes and made attempts to hold offenders accountable through the criminal and/or civil justice systems, a much higher rate of reporting and participation than average for victims of these crimes. Six (20 percent) had actually taken part in proceedings that resulted in criminal conviction of the offender. If conviction is considered the metric of success, this represents a much higher rate of success than the justice system generally delivers.

My interviewing method was unstructured, meaning that I simply allowed the conversation to unfold as my informants shared their stories. I asked what would make things right—or as right as possible—for them and what they thought the consequences should be for the offenders and bystanders. Since victims are so frequently stereotyped as vengeful, I did ask specifically about angry and vindictive feelings. I also asked for their views on forgiveness. For those who had had encounters with the formal structures of justice, I asked why they reported the crimes and what their experiences had been. Most of the interviews were recorded and transcribed; sometimes I just took notes. All of my informants gave written informed consent.

I began this project twenty years ago during a fellowship year at the Radcliffe Institute for Advanced Studies. I wrote up some preliminary findings in a paper that was published in a special issue of the journal *Violence Against Women* on restorative justice in 2005.[1] Then life intervened, in the form of illnesses and a move to an assisted-living community, followed by widowhood and then grandmotherhood. For all these reasons, the project was put on the shelf. In the last three years I have finally been able to return to it. I conducted some additional interviews, including reinterviewing three survivors with whom I had first spoken twenty years earlier, to learn how their views had evolved. During the pandemic, while I was pretty much in solitary confinement, the time finally seemed right to begin writing this book.

PART ONE

POWER

1

THE RULES OF TYRANNY

In founding a democratic republic upon law and establishing a system of checks and balances, the Founding Fathers sought to avoid the evil that they, like the ancient philosophers, called *tyranny*. They had in mind the usurpation of power by a single individual or group, or the circumvention of law by rulers for their own benefit. Much of the succeeding political debate in the United States has concerned the problem of tyranny within American society: over slaves and women, for example.

—Timothy Snyder, *On Tyranny*[1]

The *Merriam-Webster Dictionary* defines "tyranny" as "cruel and unfair treatment by people with power over others." Dictionary .com defines it as "arbitrary or unrestrained exercise of power; despotic abuse of authority." The *Cambridge English Dictionary* speaks of "government by a ruler or small group of people who have unlimited power over the people in their country or state and use it unfairly and cruelly." Common to all three definitions is the idea of power exercised without limits. Tyranny is the antithesis of the Enlightenment concepts of liberty, equality, human rights, and the rule of law. I argue in this book that tyranny is also the antithesis of justice.

Tyrannical societies are governed by the rules of dominance and subordination. These rules are quite simple: The strong do as they will because they can. The weak and vulnerable submit. Bystanders are fearfully silent, willfully blind, or willingly complicit with those in power. Those who resist risk extreme punishment: beating, imprisonment, torture, or execution. These basic rules prevail in established dictatorships, in absolute monarchies, and in territories ruled by criminal gangs and paramilitary groups. They also prevail within the domains of slavery, human trafficking, and prostitution, within some religious cults, and all too often within families. These rules can also apply within established democracies when entire groups of people (e.g., women, people of color) are excluded, de jure or de facto, from the full rights of citizenship. In this book, I mainly cite examples from the domain of gender-based violence because that is what I know best. I would propose, however, that these basic ideas about the organization of power also apply, with some variations, in many other domains of oppression, where groups of people have been historically subordinated based on attributes such as race, caste, national origin, social class, or religion.

The rule of the strong is enforced, always, by violence and the threat of violence. This is the ultimate exercise of power. Since most people will naturally resent being subjected to the control of a tyrant and some may be tempted to rebel, periodic resort to violence is always necessary to maintain the supremacy of the ruler and teach subordinate groups to know their place. All too often, however, the violence of those who rule is all but invisible. Law and custom too often support the dominance of the ruling group, and the ruling ideology may even maintain a pretense of peace and social harmony. To the extent that the violence is acknowledged, ruling ideology blames the victims for provoking it. Under such circumstances, victims of violence have no basic rights and therefore no recourse for protection and redress of wrongs. There may be laws on the books and even courts of law, but these are simply instruments of the arbitrary power of the dictator or the dominant group; therefore, there is no justice.

Methods of Coercive Control

Although violence is the ultimate method by which dominance is maintained, it is not the only one; rather, it is one of many methods of coercion used to enforce obedience and control. It is important to understand these methods, which are used worldwide, in order to understand their impact both on individual victims and on the larger society. In 1957, social scientist Albert Biderman published a "chart of coercion" based on the methods used by Chinese Communists to extract false confessions from US Air Force prisoners of war during the Korean War. At that time, these methods were mystified as some new diabolical "brainwashing" technique that the Communists had invented, but Biderman took pains to explain that these were time-tested methods that "police and inquisitors had employed for centuries."[2] In 1973, Amnesty International published an almost identical chart of coercion, based on the testimonies of torture survivors from many different cultures and autocratic regimes.[3] In 1984, a battered women's program in Duluth, Minnesota, published the "Violence Wheel," a graphic illustrating the most common methods batterers used to maintain dominance over their partners. The center of the wheel is power and control; the spokes are all the methods of coercion. The two lists are basically congruent, evidence that the features of tyranny are recognizable and the methods of maintaining it are the same, whether in the public sphere of war and governance, traditionally the world of men, or in the private sphere of intimate relationships, traditionally the world to which women are confined.

Violence does not need to be used very often; it merely needs to be convincing when it is used. There is a saying in the battered women's movement that "one good beating is good for a year." A victim may report, "I saw that look in his eyes, and I realized that he really could kill me." Thereafter, the threat of violence, or simply that look in his eyes, may be sufficient to produce displays of submission, and she will be on permanent alert for that look. A Central Intelligence Agency manual for the interrogation of detainees observes, "The threat of coercion usually weakens or destroys resistance more effectively than coercion itself."[4]

Three additional methods will reliably reduce a victim to submission: control of bodily functions, capricious enforcement of petty rules, and random intermittent rewards. Sleep deprivation may be the best-known method of controlling bodily functions: abusers disrupt and take control of the body's deep

Power and Control Wheel

Source: Domestic Abuse Intervention Programs, Duluth, MN,
www.theduluthmodel.org

rhythms that respond to daily cycles of darkness and light. Food deprivation, of course, is another. Sensory deprivation and the use of drugs to induce altered states will further break down the victim's sense of identity and bodily integrity. Control of the body may also include dictating rules for bodily hair and what the victim may wear. Extreme cases (gangs and cults; slave plantations and concentration camps) may include tattooing or branding.

These methods of control are also practiced, in less extreme forms, by people in positions of power who abuse their authority. As an eminent US federal appellate judge once told his law clerks, "I control what you read, what you write, what you eat. You don't sleep if I say so. You don't shit unless I say so. Do you understand?"[5] Apparently, he wasn't kidding. For decades this man was notorious for his abusive behavior toward his law clerks and especially for sexual harassment. Even those entrusted with implementing the rule of law can sometimes prefer the rules and methods of tyranny.

The capricious enforcement of petty and arbitrary rules is designed to break the will of the victim and to deprive her of agency. Rachel Lloyd, a survivor of sex trafficking, describes the way pimps use this method of domination:

When a pimp uses the phrase *pimps up, hos down*, he means that you need to be in the street while he walks on the sidewalk. Being *out of pocket* refers to showing disrespect for your pimp or another pimp and can apply to infractions such as looking another pimp directly in the eye, disagreeing with your pimp, or not making enough money. Punishment for breaking the rules ranges from a beating from your own pimp to being put in a *pimp circle* . . . There are myriad rules and codes—all designed to break down individual will. In the beginning, you rarely understand all the different rules, until, of course, you break one.[6]

Because the victim never knows what actions on her part might be punished, she is compelled to abandon her own initiative and simply obey. Early in the battered women's movement, this state of subjection was compared to "learned helplessness," the condition of laboratory rats unable to escape sadistic shocking by experimenters.

As any student of rat and pigeon psychology knows, however, a steady schedule of punishment is not nearly as powerful in shaping behavior as a similar schedule that tosses in a few random rewards. This is the basis of the good cop/bad cop method of obtaining confessions from prisoners. The aim of the perpetrator is to instill in his victim not only fear of death but also gratitude for permission to live.

These first four methods of coercive control are effective in breaking the victim's will. But for many tyrants, having a submissive victim is not sufficient; they demand a *willing* victim. For this, it is necessary to break the victim's spirit. Three additional methods are required. The first is isolation, fracturing relationships with others who might offer solace and support. Batterers, for example, may demand that their partners stop visiting their friends and families, often with jealous accusations of infidelity. The second method is degradation, dirtying the victim so that she will feel repulsive to herself and to others and forcing her to do things that she finds humiliating and disgusting. The last and most toxic method of all is forcing the victim to violate her own moral codes by betraying or harming those she loves. These last three methods work primarily by inducing not fear but rather shame.

Shame, like fear, is an intense emotion that creates indelible memories. Unlike fear, shame is a social emotion, a signal of threat not to life but to human connection. It is a response to rejection, ridicule, or ostracism. It is also a response to violation of boundaries, to being stripped or seen naked. Most people can remember vividly moments of acute embarrassment, feeling a wish to hide, to "crawl into a hole and die." This is ordinary shame. It can be relieved by friendly eye contact and shared laughter, and it functions ultimately to preserve community by setting group norms of behavior. The malignant shame of people subjected to methods of coercive control is of a different order of magnitude. The wish to die is not metaphorical but all too real. Victims feel permanently dirty, disgusting, and defiled. If, under duress, they have hurt others, they often feel such intense guilt and shame that they believe they no longer deserve to live.

The postures of shame—the bowed head, slumped shoulders, and averted gaze—are recognizable across cultures. They are similar to the submissive displays of other mammals and are probably hardwired in the same way. Tyrants and dominant groups will often demand these postural displays as tokens of submission. The Rolling Stones famously sang of triumph over the "girl" who must do just what she's told and keep her eyes down.[7] Under the dominion of slavery and lynch law, Black people could be whipped, branded, burned, or worse for failure to perform these gestures of humiliation. After being beaten, enslaved people would sometimes be required to kneel before their masters and thank them. As interpreted by Black sociology scholar Orlando Patterson, the submissive displays of the enslaved convey a condition of "social death" in which life itself is utterly contingent on the will of the master.[8] The legacy of enslavement still lives in "The Talk," instructions for surviving an encounter with a police officer that Black parents feel obliged to give to their children: bow your head, look down, obey instructions, don't make any sudden moves, don't argue or protest, and say "Yes, sir" and "No, sir" in a soft voice.

The methods that enforce and maintain tyranny are the same worldwide. They are taught by one clandestine police force to another, and they are taught and practiced informally against subordinated and marginalized groups in many ordinary police forces. They are taught in the organized criminal gangs that traffic in drugs and guns. They are taught in human trafficking and the sex trade. Pimps, prison guards, cult leaders, batterers, and perpetrators of incest practice these methods. They are used worldwide because they work.

Rules for Bystanders

So far, in elaborating the rules of tyranny, I have spoken only of victims and perpetrators. But in order to terrorize an entire group, it's not necessary to inflict extreme punishment on everyone. Rather, the violent enforcement of dominance against a few people, especially anyone who dares to protest, will serve as a warning to the rest of the group to shut up and keep their heads down, literally and metaphorically. Ambitious souls who might be tempted to resist can also be co-opted. Tyrants frequently cultivate elite fraternities within religious, political, military, or frankly criminal organizations, as well as within the police. These secret societies become the enforcers of the tyrant's dictatorial powers. Often these elite groups have elaborate rituals of initiation, in which many of the methods of coercive control are imposed on recruits, including the demand for unconditional loyalty. In return, those who join the fraternities learn how to become predators themselves and are rewarded with a share of the resulting bounty, both in wealth and in women's bodies.

Tyrannical regimes also cultivate attitudes of cynicism, indifference, and narrow egotism among the general public, encouraging people to look out for their own skins only and to look the other way when their neighbors are hurt. By undermining any sense of community or the common good, the rulers keep their subordinate populations isolated and under control. These regimes also foster corruption, on both a petty and a grand scale, implicitly encouraging people to seek whatever advantage they can over their fellow citizens. As journalist Masha Gessen explains, in autocratic regimes, being close to power is the best, and sometimes the only, way to acquire wealth, and wealth is used in turn to maintain power. "The system cannot exist without corruption," they write, "because corruption is its fuel, its social glue, and its instrument of control." One might also think of corruption as an autocratic system's social *solvent*, dissolving the people's trust in one another and in the rule of law. Gessen adds, "Anyone who enters the system becomes complicit in the corruption, which means everyone is always in some ways outside the law."[9] Those who participate in minor corruptions such as bribery tend to rationalize their participation in a lawless system by asserting that everybody does it and that only fools believe in such public virtues as honesty.

Gessen also points out that tyrants and their apologists in autocratic regimes lie constantly, not so much to deny their crimes (although that is one reason) as to assert that reality is whatever the tyrant says it is. Faced with a tyrant's constant barrage of lies, gaslighting, and propaganda, many ordinary people will simply tune out. When seeking the truth becomes too dangerous or just too exhausting, it is tempting simply to retreat from any form of public engagement, focusing only on the narrowest private concerns. The more ordinary people withdraw their attention from the public sphere, the more the tyrant gains in his claim to absolute power, not merely over the law but over truth itself.[10]

Those who live under the rules of tyranny are thus faced with a range of possibilities as bystanders. They can choose to become accomplices and followers of the tyrant and gain the benefits of active collusion in a corrupt system; they can become silent witnesses who are aware of abuses of power but keep quiet out of fear or indifference; or they can simply retreat into a stance of unknowing, feeling that they are powerless to make a difference in any event. All these levels of collusion can be rationalized as just "going along to get along," simply accepting that this is the way the world is. One can sympathize with the dilemma of bystanders, for few will have the courage to seek out the truth, to speak up, or to intervene on behalf of victims, knowing the kinds of punishments they may risk themselves. It is only too easy to say, "It's none of my business, and anyway, there's nothing I can do about it."

The situation is even more complicated for those who live under democratic governments, as in the United States, but where the rules of tyranny still apply, in varying degrees, to people who have been historically subordinated, both at home and in colonial empires. Historian Michael Rothberg has coined the term "implicated subjects" for those who are neither perpetrators nor victims but should not simply be considered "passive bystanders" because they benefit, knowingly or not, from the oppression of others, and their actions, or failure to act, help to perpetuate the social structures of inequality. Implicated subjects, in Rothberg's view, can be part of a "transmission belt of domination." Even if ignorant of the violent crimes and the methods of coercive control that perpetuate the rules of tyranny, they are morally compromised because they enjoy privileges derived indirectly from the subordination of others. Therefore, even if not directly involved as witnesses, they share in the social responsibility for making things right. "'Modes of implication'— entanglements in historical and present-day injustices—are complex, multifaceted, and sometimes contradictory," he writes, "but are nonetheless essential to confront in the pursuit of justice."[11]

For those who are the most directly victimized, the complicity and silence of bystanders—friends, relatives, and neighbors, not to mention officials of the law—feel like a profound betrayal, for this is what isolates them and abandons them to their fates. Survivors can perhaps accept the fact that some people are predators or psychopaths who seek absolute power. But what about all those who collaborate: the enablers, the apologists, those who profit from the subjection of others? What about all those who collude implicitly: the people who prefer not to know the truth or choose not to help, the people who say, "It's none of my business," and those who are just looking out for themselves? What about those who blame the victims for disturbing the peace? What about those who are tasked with implementing justice but instead ally themselves with the powerful? Often, survivors will feel the bitterness of these betrayals more deeply even than the direct harms inflicted by perpetrators. This is a theme we will hear repeatedly throughout this book in the testimonies of survivors.

No tyrant is omnipotent, no matter how grandiose his claims. The regime of tyranny cannot be maintained without the active complicity or passive acquiescence of many other people. Once bystanders begin to take a righteous stand in support of survivors, the power of the tyrant begins to crumble. For this reason, repairing the harms of tyranny first of all requires bystanders and the larger community to recognize their own moral responsibility and to take action in solidarity with those who have been harmed. They must find the courage to seek out and acknowledge the truth, to overcome their fear and cynicism, to denounce the crimes of tyranny, and to ally with survivors in the name of human dignity. It is this reconciliation with the larger community that many survivors seek when they speak of justice.

If the rules of tyranny are inherently unjust, then other rules must be invented under which people can live in community and justice can be done. The next chapter explores the nature of the social compact that is required to create a basic moral foundation for justice.

2

THE RULES OF EQUALITY

We are caught in an inescapable network of mutuality, tied in a seamless garment of destiny.

—Martin Luther King Jr.[1]

What is justice? According to the *Merriam-Webster Dictionary*, justice means fair treatment. The *Oxford English Dictionary* concurs. The *Cambridge English Dictionary* lists as synonyms "equity," "fairness," and "impartiality." The *Simple English Wikipedia* expands on the definition, calling it "a concept in ethics and law based on egalitarian ideas that all people have equal moral worth." By definition, then, the foundation of justice is the democratic principle of equality.

Under tyranny, social relationships are characterized by dominance and subordination and maintained by the methods of coercion displayed in the "Violence Wheel" graphic in

Chapter 1. Under these rules, there are winners and losers. With equality, by contrast, social relationships are characterized by mutuality and maintained by cooperation, as displayed in the "Nonviolence Wheel." Everyone has an equal voice. Everyone is entitled to respect and care. Power and responsibility are shared. Decisions are made by mutual consent and compromise. Disputes are resolved through negotiation. Relationships are governed by principles of trust and fairness and bounded by the rule of law. All members of the community share a commitment to the common good and to certain inalienable rights. Under these rules, ideally, there are only winners; everyone stands to gain freedom, prosperity, and safety.

Just as there is no absolute tyranny, there is no perfect democracy. The principle of equality is an ideal, never fully realized. There will always be some inequalities in social resources such as wealth and education. Some relationships, such as those between adults and children, are inherently unequal. Still, social relationships in a democratic system aspire to be governed by a principle of mutuality and founded on practices of cooperation, respect, and fairness rather than assertions of power and control.

The concept of equality as the foundation of justice follows an Enlightenment philosophical tradition that recognizes the human right to liberty as axiomatic and considers human equality to be the basis of society and governance. Modern philosopher John Rawls, in his treatise *A Theory of Justice*, follows in this tradition. In the first chapter of this comprehensive work, he writes that justice is "the first virtue of social institutions" and "the fundamental charter of a well-ordered human

NONVIOLENCE

NEGOTIATION AND FAIRNESS
Seeking mutually satisfying resolutions to conflict · accepting change · being willing to compromise.

NON-THREATENING BEHAVIOR
Talking and acting so that she feels safe and comfortable expressing herself and doing things.

ECONOMIC PARTNERSHIP
Making money decisions together · making sure both partners benefit from financial arrangements.

RESPECT
Listening to her non-judgmentally · being emotionally affirming and understanding · valuing opinions.

EQUALITY

SHARED RESPONSIBILITY
Mutually agreeing on a fair distribution of work · making family decisions together.

TRUST AND SUPPORT
Supporting her goals in life · respecting her right to her own feelings, friends, activities and opinions.

RESPONSIBLE PARENTING
Sharing parental responsibilities · being a positive nonviolent role model for the children.

HONESTY AND ACCOUNTABILITY
Accepting responsibility for self · acknowledging past use of violence · admitting being wrong · communicating openly and truthfully.

NONVIOLENCE

Equality Wheel
Source: Domestic Abuse Intervention Programs, Duluth, MN, www.theduluthmodel.org

association," and he sets forth the proposition that justice should be understood as fairness. He argues that the idea of justice as fairness is both conceptually rational and easy to understand intuitively. Young children readily recognize the concept of fairness as soon as they begin to play games in groups. The rules of the game apply to everyone equally, and children who grow up in freedom will cry, "No fair!" when anyone violates the implicit social contract of their games. Building on the social contract theories of John Locke, Jean-Jacques Rousseau, and Immanuel Kant, Professor Rawls proposes that the concept of justice as fairness "constitutes the most appropriate moral basis for a democratic society."[2]

Justice and the rule of law can be understood as a way of balancing the democratic claims of liberty and equality and protecting the safety of all citizens. Everyone has an equal right to life and liberty, but any one person's liberty ends where it infringes on the rights of others. No one has the right to coerce another person to submit to his will. For this reason, in a just society, the law forbids using the methods of coercive control against other people. Violence, threats, and harassment are crimes.

A question then arises: How does a just society respond when laws are broken and crimes are committed? The institutions of the justice system are devised for this purpose. Special representatives of the community are called upon to implement justice: police, who are called upon to intervene and investigate when laws are broken and who have a monopoly on the legitimate use of force; prosecutors, who represent the society in presenting evidence of crimes in courts of law; and judges, who are called upon to rule fairly and impartially on how the laws are applied and to determine the consequences for those who have broken them.

The powers invested in these professionals are immense and easily abused. It is for this good reason that so many protections for those suspected of crimes are built into the United States' Constitution and criminal laws. Unfortunately, these protections are not balanced by corresponding protections for those who have been harmed. The perspectives of crime victims have no formal representation before the institutions of law enforcement and law.

Even in a democracy, the interests of victims are not the same as the interests of the state. In the United States, for example, police have immense discretion over how seriously they investigate crimes and whether to arrest suspects, and prosecutors have immense discretion over whether or not to file criminal charges. In practice, some victims are considered more deserving of these efforts than others, based on attributes such as race, social class, and gender. Even when suspects are arrested and charged with crimes, most cases are never presented in court; rather, they are resolved by a "plea bargain," a negotiation between the prosecutor and the attorney for the defense. The victim is not included and has no say in any of these decisions; sometimes she is not even informed about them. If the case does proceed to trial, the victim is obliged to submit to hostile questioning by the defense attorney, who will make every effort to humiliate and discredit her. In this manner, the existing institutions of justice fall far short of the ideal of fairness in the treatment of crime victims.

Traditional Institutions of Justice

Probably sometime in the 1980s, in the early days of the Victims of Violence Program, I took a daylong course at the Annual Meeting of the American Psychiatric Association. Dr. Phil Resnick, an eminent forensic psychiatrist, was lecturing on how to testify in court as an expert witness. Sometimes (though not often) our patients did seek justice in court, and I wanted to know how to testify effectively on their behalf if need be. To introduce his subject, Dr. Resnick projected onto a huge screen a picture of two groups of Appalachian mountain men, scowling and looking formidable with their huge mustaches and their rifles across their knees. These were the legendary Hatfields and McCoys, notorious for their multigenerational blood feud.

"Why do we have courts of law?" Dr. Resnick asked. He allowed that some people might believe that we have courts of law in order to establish the truth or in order to mete out justice. These were naïvely idealistic notions, according to Dr. Resnick. The real reason we have courts, he proposed, is in order to resolve disputes without recourse to firearms. Courts of law in the United States, he warned, are hostile territories where adversaries may use any cruel or threatening tactics short of physical attack in order to prevail.

The image of these armed white men has remained with me over the years. It seems to me now that our traditional legal system was indeed designed to resolve conflicts between white men, and only white men: those who had standing as citizens in the early years of the republic. Our legal system was not designed initially to redress the harms done to women or to enslaved or Indigenous people. Often, in fact, it has been an active instrument of those harms. So perhaps it is not surprising that both women and the descendants of enslaved peoples remain to this day deeply alienated from the legal system.

In our system of criminal law, the state, not the victim, is actually considered the injured party, and it is the state, not the victim, that has the exclusive right to take action against a criminal offender. This is a cornerstone of Enlightenment legal theory and is a basic premise of modern democracies. In this conception of justice, the person who is actually harmed has very little part to play in the process. Her role is simply as a witness. The drama is all in the conflict between prosecution and defense, which Dr. Resnick described as warfare without firearms. As one of my informants, Mary Walsh, a survivor of domestic violence, put it, "Be prepared for the fact that you will simply be a 'cog in something turning' and you had better learn early on not to take things personally. Even though you will know more about the facts of the case, since you are only a witness, you will not be consulted. For your own peace of mind, be prepared to throw any illusions about 'justice' you might have had out the window."

Why are crime victims relegated to such a marginal role in our justice system? The answer seems to be an expectation that victims will be too angry, too irrational, too fixated on retribution to be trusted. In the words of Arieh Neier, a leading contemporary human rights advocate, "In a society of law, we say it is not up to the individual victims to exercise vengeance, but rather up to society to demonstrate respect for the victim, for the one who suffered, by rendering the victimizer accountable."[3] The presumption that the state will be more dispassionate and fairer than the victim is rarely questioned. It is simply taken for granted that victims will crave revenge and that allowing victims any active role in the procedures of justice will lead inevitably, at best, to the end of due process and, at worst, to endless feuding, where vigilantes take the law into their own hands.

The righteous anger of women and other subordinated groups, which violates dominant norms of compliant and willing submission, is always particularly threatening. Anger is a most unwelcome sentiment from the crime victims whom the dominant community would most prefer to ignore. The victim's passionate indignation is commonly perceived as a disruptive force, disturbing the peace and comfort of the bystanders who are called upon to redress the victim's wrongs. Moral and legal philosopher Martha Nussbaum names anger as one of the "vices of victimhood." She does make a distinction between anger that is "forward facing," rightfully seeking redress of a wrong, and anger that is purely retributive, seeking to inflict pain on the offender, and she recognizes that most victims will feel some mixture of the two.[4] But naming anger as a vice comes uncomfortably close to shaming the victim, which is all too common.

The general societal condemnation of victims' anger is so reflexive and deep as to render it taboo. Writer Susan Jacoby describes the operation of this taboo in the expectation that victims of even the most atrocious crimes must establish the purity of their motives before seeking redress by first making a humble ritual declaration that they wish only for "justice, not revenge."[5] When groups who have been victimized organize to call attention to the violence directed at them, they have been historically vilified as "troublemakers" and persecuted on suspicion of desire to subvert the social order by means of violence. This was true a century ago in the labor movement, it was true sixty years ago in the civil rights movement, and it is true again today.

In fact, victims' anger has everything to do with the way their community responds to the wrongs inflicted upon them. Retributive anger—what I would call blind rage or humiliated fury—is what people feel when they are alone and abandoned to their fates. The wish to retaliate is born of isolation and help-lessness. In an essay titled "Revenge Is Sour," George Orwell explains, "Properly speaking, there is no such thing as revenge. Revenge is an act, which you want to commit when you are pow-erless and because you are powerless: as soon as the sense of im-potence is removed, the desire evaporates also. Who would not have jumped for joy, in 1940, at the thought of seeing SS officers kicked and humiliated? But when the thing becomes possible, it is merely pathetic and disgusting."[6]

When the community rallies to the victim's support, venge-ful feelings are transformed into shared righteous indignation, which can be a powerful source of energy for repair. It is only when victims are denied their fair measure of justice that their anger can fester as helpless rage. Legal philosopher Jeffrie Mur-phy invokes Greek myth as a narrative metaphor for the proper foundation of justice. Athena, the goddess of wisdom, trans-forms the Furies from persecuting monsters into Eumenides (kindly ones) by including rather than banishing them. Expand-ing on this vision, Murphy argues that the crime victim's re-sentment and indignation are in fact valid feelings that deserve social recognition and respect. He recognizes that this passion can be excessive, but then, he argues, what passion cannot?[7]

Rather than ceding to common prejudices and fears about victims, a truly fair system needs to find a better way of including them in the workings of justice.

The Idea of a Moral Community

Legal scholar Ross London has seen the US justice system from many perspectives. In the course of his career, he has served as a prosecutor, a defense attorney, and a municipal court judge. In his book *Crime, Punishment, and Restorative Justice*, he proposes new ideas of justice that give greater attention to crime victims. Professor London elaborates on social contract theory with the idea of a moral community, which he defines as "those who are bound by the rules of social reciprocity."[8] A concept derived from the sociobiology of altruism, the moral community originates in kinship networks and expands to wider social groups in which belonging is predicated upon trust that members will respect a mutual moral code. When that trust is violated, the moral community is expected to share the victim's feelings of hurt and outrage, to mobilize to help the victim, and to hold the perpetrator accountable. By these actions, the community affirms the victim's belonging and conditions the offender's continued membership on convincing displays of contrition and willingness to make amends.

London conceptualizes the origins of justice in the alliance between the victim and the moral community, which rallies to enforce a code of mutuality. He describes the fundamental breach of trust and sense of injustice that occur when the community fails to hold perpetrators accountable for their crimes. He writes, "Victims of crime whose suffering is regarded as solely their private misfortune are likely to feel isolated and, indeed, disrespected by the moral community. Only when a victim's resentment and demand for justice are shared by the group can the victim feel restored to full membership in the moral community."[9]

The concepts of trust and mutuality as the foundations of justice and moral community make sense not only legally and philosophically but also psychologically. In his classic work *Childhood and Society*, developmental psychologist Erik Erikson describes trust as the foundation of human psychological development. On the basis of secure attachment to a reliable caretaker, children develop the capacities for autonomy and initiative, young adults develop a sense of identity and the capacities for intimacy and caretaking, and mature adults develop the virtue of integrity. Each generation of children depends in turn for its survival, health, and happiness on the ability to trust in the caring and integrity of adults.[10]

The interlocking of the generations gives rise to a felt sense of interdependence. Though the relationship of infant to adult caretaker could not be more unequal in terms of power, nevertheless it can be considered a foundational social contract, for it is surely a relationship of reciprocity that gives benefits to both. The infant's first smile, at about six weeks of age, evokes spontaneous delight and an outpouring of affection, a dopamine response that is hardwired in even the most exhausted and sleep-deprived parent. These fundamental attachment bonds form the psychological basis for trust, and this in turn forms the basis for human sociability and for a moral community based on a code of fairness and mutuality.[11]

The idea of a moral community resonates in particular with the testimony of survivors. I would use the term broadly, as a community to which the individual belongs and which she trusts to come to her aid when she is hurt. When this does not happen, a victim of a violent crime feels abandoned by her community, and her trust and sense of belonging are deeply violated. The victim feels isolated and cast out. Too often, the result is a profound sense of dishonor, a disgraced identity. In her victim impact statement, writer Chanel Miller, one of the rare sexual assault victims who dared to report the crime and undergo the full rigors of a public trial, wrote to the judge, "In newspapers my name was 'unconscious intoxicated woman,' ten syllables, and nothing more than that. For a while I believed that was all I was. I had to force myself to relearn my real name, my identity. To relearn that . . . I am not just a drunk victim at a frat party found behind a dumpster . . . I am a human being who has been irreversibly hurt."[12] This is what is meant by a disgraced identity.

Victim impact statements such as Chanel Miller's are a recent innovation in US criminal law, one of the few designed to give victims a greater voice in the proceedings. First recommended by the Presidential Task Force on Victims of Crime in 1982, this reform, now implemented in most states, allows victims of violent crimes to speak or write directly to judges in the sentencing phase of criminal trials, after the facts of the case have been established beyond a reasonable doubt and the defendant has pled or been found guilty. In 1991, the Supreme Court ruled that such testimony was admissible and did not violate the Constitution. This would seem like rather a small gesture of inclusion. It does not in any way challenge the primary role of the state in prosecution, the adversarial system for arriving at a determination of guilt, or the ultimate discretion of judges in sentencing. In all these matters, victims still remain "a cog in something turning."

Nevertheless, both liberals and traditionalists have objected to these statements, with the expectation that victims who are allowed to speak in their own voice will inevitably demand extreme punishment of the offender. I sometimes wonder whether those who stereotype victims in this way have actually ever read an impact statement. I have read quite a number of them. I am often struck by the contrast between the formality of legal proceedings and the ordinariness and humility of these statements. Many are handwritten. Most writers simply seek to be seen and heard as individuals who have been hurt rather than as case file numbers. They want the judges, as representatives of the moral community, to understand how they and their families have suffered and how their suffering continues. Some mention that the perpetrators' families must be suffering too. Here are some examples (with names disguised):

Dear Judge, I was very angry at everybody because of what Larry did to me. I am very afraid of Larry. There was nights when I couldn't sleep because I was thinking about what happened. I would like Larry to confess to my mother what he did to me because my mother doesn't believe me. I would like you to give Larry the punishment that fits the crime that he did to me.

I have talked to counselors, police, doctors, nurses. I've been examined and photographed and had my dignity torn from me! I've had to tell my children what happened to me. How does a mother find words, age appropriate words, for her kids so they can handle it? What age appropriate words do you use for rape?

Your Honor, I have had a very hard time becoming close to people and opening up to them for the fear of being violated again since the night Wesley B. made me a victim of his crime. Both my family and I had to try and cope with the publicity and obscene comments this case has brought upon us. I have been robbed of my innocence as a child and have been pushed to grow up all in one night.

Critics of impact statements such as these also presume that judges will be swayed by their sympathy for victims to impose excessively harsh sentences (though this has not turned out to be the case).[13] Judges, in their view, should be above such sentiments. I would argue, to the contrary, that judges, as representatives of the moral community, should affirm their solidarity with victims of crime, once a crime has been proven. This is quite different from showing bias toward either the accused or the complaining witness before the facts have been established according to the rules of due process. When a jury has found that a crime has been committed, the institutions of justice must ally with the survivor. Trust is rebuilt only when victims see that those in a position of authority have listened to them and share in their righteous indignation. So often that is the main thing they seek.

Moral philosopher Bernard Williams argues that the capacity to feel indignation on behalf of others is the basis of an important social bond. Rather than as a toxic passion that ought to be suppressed, he views resentment and indignation as a potential source of empathy and connection. He explains that people are capable of reacting with indignation not only when their own honor is violated but also when they witness the dishonoring of others. These "shared sentiments," according to Williams, "serve to bind people together in a community of feeling."[14]

Justice in some form is necessary in order to heal the victim's profound sense of humiliation and abandonment by her moral community. For this reason, the pursuit of justice, with its promise to restore respect for the victim's humanity, must be a major part of the process of healing from psychological trauma. In standing by the survivor, implicated bystanders reclaim their own moral standing. As the survivor puts down her burden of shame, the community puts down its own burden of guilt for its previous indifference or, worse, its complicity with the perpetrator. In restoring honor to the survivor, the moral community also restores its own honor.

3

PATRIARCHY

Different things are valued in different cultures; but whatever is
valued, women are not that. If bottom is bottom, look across time
and space, and women are whom you will find there.

—Catharine A. MacKinnon, *Feminism Unmodified*[1]

The most widespread and enduring form of tyranny is patriarchy. A social system of male dominance and female subordination has prevailed over millennia and still prevails to a greater
or lesser degree in countries throughout the modern world. It
coexists with many different forms of government, from tribal
monarchies to totalitarian dictatorships to constitutional democracies like the United States. Patriarchy is a prime example
of the many ways in which the rules and methods of tyranny
can pervade a society, from its most intimate relationships to its
institutions of governance, law, and justice.

Male supremacy, like other forms of tyranny, is enforced, ultimately, by violence. The data on this point, gathered internationally by agencies of the United Nations, are compelling. Violence against women is one of the most common human rights violations in the world.[2] In the United States, repeated nationwide epidemiological surveys report that about 20 percent of women have been victims of rape. Girls and young women ages twelve to twenty-four are at the highest risk. The statistics are even worse for Black, brown, Indigenous, and lesbian women.[3] Other prosperous countries where similar studies have been conducted have similar statistics. In countries at peace, the perpetrators of violence are primarily private citizens known to the victim: acquaintances and family members rather than uniformed agents of the state. In wartime, the prevalence of rape skyrockets because armies use rape as a tool of conquest and ethnic cleansing, as a means to humiliate the enemy by defiling their women and girls (and sometimes their men and boys as well). Historical accounts of mass rape in conflict zones worldwide going back to antiquity suggest that about the only thing that warring groups of men can agree upon is that victory gives them permission to assault the other side's women and children or take them prisoner as sex slaves. Reports just since the mid-twentieth century have documented this practice during invasions or civil conflicts in the following countries: Vietnam, Cambodia, Indonesia, Afghanistan, Bangladesh, Myanmar, Iraq, Syria, Libya, Sudan, Uganda, Rwanda, Democratic Republic of the Congo, Cyprus, Bosnia, Colombia, and, most recently, Ukraine. This is by no means an exhaustive list.[4]

Rape could be considered the signal crime of male supremacy, a pure enactment of power for its own sake. Often celebrated by men in groups (fraternity brothers, paramilitaries), it sexualizes the performance of dominance and submission and teaches women and girls to know their place. Its prevalence is so high, especially among young people, that one can hardly consider it a deviant act. When US college students respond to confidential surveys, about one woman in four acknowledges being coerced into sexual relations, and roughly 5 to 10 percent of young men acknowledge having "taken advantage" of a woman sexually at least once.[5] Yet rape, for all its complexities and no matter how harmful, is in some ways the least complex form of gender oppression, because it is often a single event, and after the ordeal is over, the victim is able to escape.

Other forms of sexual exploitation, such as sex trafficking and workplace harassment, involve repeated violations. This means that a relationship of coercive control has been established, making it difficult for the victim to escape. Fear of physical retaliation or economic dependency, or both, may entrap her. Such relationships begin to deform the victim's personality as she tries simultaneously to embrace the performance of submission and to hide some part of herself that still rebels. Still more complicated are those domestic violence relationships where expressions of love are fused with demands for obedience, where the victim may also be economically dependent on the perpetrator, and where perpetrator and victim share a home and children. In these situations, victims under duress may become passive or complicit bystanders as well as victims. Battered women, for instance, may sometimes be too terrorized to intervene when they witness abuse of their children, or they may even blame the children for provoking the violence. We will hear such stories in the course of this book. This is how the methods of tyranny compel people to violate their own moral codes and to betray those whom they love.

Most complex of all are those forms of sexual abuse where the victims are children and adolescents. These, too, are not rare events. According to the Centers for Disease Control and Prevention, approximately one in four girls and one in thirteen boys in the United States have experienced sexual abuse.[6] For both girls and boys, the great majority of abusers are men whom they know and trust: family members, teachers, sports coaches, and religious leaders. In one random-sample survey of nine hundred adult women, 16 percent reported childhood sexual abuse by a relative, and 4.5 percent reported abuse by a father or stepfather.[7] It might be argued that these US data reflect a permissive, decadent culture where traditional patriarchal customs have broken down, but in fact one of the strongest correlates of father-daughter incest is patriarchal violence.[8]

While the methods of tyranny, applied to adults, may break a victim's spirit, applied to children, they create a broken identity. When the abuser is the very person on whom the child depends for care and protection, she learns from an early age that people who claim to love her are going to hurt her and that being hurt is the price of love. Such early violations of trust and safe attachment damage the formation of a coherent sense of self, embodied in space, continuous in time, and deserving of love. Survivors may say things like "I don't exist" or "My body doesn't belong to me," or they may be unable to recognize themselves in a mirror.

In clinical terms, these would be called the dissociative experiences of depersonalization and derealization. Neurobiological studies of survivors of childhood abuse and neglect demonstrate a literal disconnection between parts of the brain that are ordinarily networked to form the foundation of self-awareness, linking perception of the body, recognition of emotions, memory of the past, and a sense of possibility in the future.[9] French writer Vanessa Springora, a survivor of sexual abuse by a celebrated literary figure, describes her experiences in these terms: "I was disappearing, evaporating, slipping away. As though my soul was leaking through the pores of my skin."[10]

As the abused child grows into adulthood, these lasting injuries compromise her ability to form relationships of trust, intimacy, and mutuality. They also damage her ability to protect herself, leaving her vulnerable to repeated abuse. My good friend and colleague, psychiatrist and researcher Frank Putnam, headed up a study that has followed a group of eighty-four sexually abused girls for over thirty years, from the time the abuse was first confirmed by child protective services, when the girls were on average eleven years old, until the present, when many have had children and even grandchildren of their own. These kids had a terrible time as adolescents and young adults. They were more likely than their peers to experience teen pregnancy, to drop out of school, and to be diagnosed with serious mental health problems like depression, posttraumatic stress disorder, and substance abuse. Suicide attempts were common.[11]

Survivors of childhood abuse are also highly likely to become victims of rape, sex trafficking, or intimate partner violence.[12] They may be invisible to most people in their communities, but apparently they are easy for predators to spot. As a pimp explains, in describing what he looks for when he recruits young women for prostitution, "Beauty, yes. Sexual expertise: somewhat. That can be taught easier than you think. What is important above all is obedience. And how do you get obedience? You get women who have had sex with their fathers, their uncles, their brothers—you know, someone they love and fear and do not dare to defy."[13] Feminist writer Andrea Dworkin describes incest as "boot camp" for prostitution.[14]

These are the afflictions born of women's oppression. Some of these burdens are carried from generation to generation.[15] Anyone who works with abused kids or adult survivors has encountered families in which domination is considered a male entitlement and abuse is repeated from one generation to the next. We will hear from some survivors who grew up in such families in the course of this book. Fortunately, however, there is good evidence that the majority of survivors of childhood abuse, both boys and girls, do not abuse their children.[16] Many are determined that the "cycle of abuse" will stop with them. For many, this will be the only kind of justice within their power to achieve. Any form of accountability for their abusers will remain out of reach.

Impunity

Many layers of custom, secrecy, and denial defend the crimes of patriarchy. In effect, they are crimes of impunity. A recent

United Nations report described the problem in these terms: "States worldwide are failing to implement in full the international standards on violence against women. . . . When the State fails to hold the perpetrators of violence accountable, this not only encourages further abuses, it also gives the message that male violence against women is acceptable or normal."[17] Psychologist and survivor Jennifer Freyd speaks of "institutional betrayal" to describe the experience of survivors who vainly seek redress from the authorities or who dare not even seek redress because they know that the pursuit of justice will only make matters worse for them.[18]

In the United States, for example, rape is nominally considered a serious crime, a felony. However, in most cases, victims are too terrified or too ashamed to tell anyone at first, much less to report the crime to the police. They are ashamed because of widespread social attitudes that victims "asked for it," and they are well aware that the police may share those attitudes. In the United States, studies estimate that no more than 20 percent of rape incidents are reported to police.[19] Those victims who do report rarely find help or solace. As part of a project called "The Presence of Justice," the *Atlantic* magazine recently published a 2019 feature article titled "An Epidemic of Disbelief," documenting all the ways that law enforcement fails to follow up on reports of sexual assault. The most damning evidence was the thousands upon thousands of untested "rape kits," semen specimens collected from victims in hospital emergency rooms, that were left to gather dust in police warehouses.[20] Along with this physical evidence of indifference and neglect, the reporter, Barbara Bradley Hagerty, documented a pervasive and tenacious belief among police officers that most reports of rape are simply not credible. She described "a subterranean river of chauvinism, where the fate of a rape case usually depends on the detective's view of the victim—not the perpetrator."

Of the few cases that are reported to law enforcement, even fewer will lead to arrest, prosecution, and conviction. Recent reviews of attrition in the criminal justice system estimate that perhaps 1 to 5 percent of all rapes are actually prosecuted, and 0 to 5 percent of all rapes result in a guilty plea or conviction.[21] For sexual abuse of children, the reporting rate is so low to begin with that, with comparable attrition, impunity is basically assured. Jane Manning, an attorney who works with sexual assault victims to help them navigate the criminal justice system, writes, "I witness this failure again and again. The survivors I serve have reported sexual assaults to law enforcement all around the country, only to find that investigators routinely fail to conduct proper victim interviews, to retrieve probative video footage, to interview crucial witnesses, to investigate the perpetrator's background to see if he has committed similar crimes, to preserve relevant digital or paper records or to conduct other basic investigative steps."[22]

Manning adds that when investigators fail to pursue rape cases properly, prosecutors will then decline to pursue these cases on the grounds that there is not enough evidence. Prosecutors also tend to decline cases of date rape or acquaintance rape, which comprise the majority of cases, when victims do not fit the stereotypical image of "innocence"—that is, they are not young, white, blond, demure, and virginal. They will rationalize this choice on the grounds that juries will be prejudiced against all but the most "perfect" victims. Prosecutors' success is judged according to the percentage of cases they win, and since winning rape cases is not a sure thing, many will avoid taking the risk, even if they view the victim's complaint as justified. The victim has no say in the matter; if the police fail to investigate, or the prosecutor declines to present the case in court, she has no recourse. As a practical matter, then, our criminal justice system utterly fails to address rape and child sexual abuse as serious crimes.

In her memoir and manifesto, *Is Rape a Crime?*, writer Michelle Bowdler describes both how her own case was ignored and how law enforcement generally neglects cases of sexual assault. She writes,

> If most of the people who either write or are charged with enforcing our laws equate rape with sex rather than violence, and sex is considered a male need and not to be challenged, then rape . . . will continue being a crime for which there are few consequences. Instead, rape and sexual assault are framed as accidents, misunderstandings, and the fantasies of women (and children) who don't understand the rules they must live by, including the rule that the perpetrator must be given a pass.[23]

Note the word "misunderstanding." It will appear again throughout the course of this book. It is one of the most common defenses employed when women do actually dare to speak up.

For those few cases that actually reach the courts, victims can expect a prolonged ordeal in an adversarial system that will subject them to hostile public scrutiny at a time when they most need care and social support to heal. The requirements of legal proceedings seem almost perfectly designed to aggravate the symptoms of posttraumatic stress. Victims need to establish a sense of power and control over their lives; the court requires them to submit to a complex set of rules and bureaucratic procedures that they may not understand and over which they have no control. Victims need time for recovery; the court sets the timetable for justice, which repeatedly disrupts their lives and is often protracted over many months or years. Victims need an opportunity to tell their stories in their own way; the court requires them to respond on the witness stand to a set of direct questions from the prosecutor and then to endure cross-examination by the defense attorney. Victims often need to control or limit their exposure to specific reminders of the trauma; the court requires them to relive their experiences in great detail. Victims often fear direct interaction with their perpetrators; the court requires a face-to-face confrontation with the accused. For all these reasons, it is common for victims of sexual violence to speak of their encounters with the justice system as a "second rape."[24]

In criminal court, the defendant is presumed to be innocent until proven guilty beyond a reasonable doubt. These two cornerstones of criminal law, the presumption of innocence and the requirement for a very high standard of proof, are designed to tip the scales of justice in favor of criminal defendants, in recognition of the tremendous imbalance of power between individual citizens and the state. But no equivalent consideration is given to the safety and well-being of crime victims who bear witness in court, despite the very real imbalance of power that so often obtains between victim and perpetrator. Many victims will decline to testify for fear of retaliation by the perpetrator, his friends, or his family. Others decline because they know that awaiting them in court is a theater of shame. In the case of rape, the presumption of innocence for the accused often translates into a simple presumption that the accuser is lying, and victims often feel that they, rather than the perpetrators, are on trial. For all these reasons, the formal structures of criminal justice are effectively closed to most victims.

What survivors need from their communities is a commitment to listen to their stories with an open mind and with care and compassion rather than skepticism and scorn. There is, of course, such a thing as a false accusation, but in the matter of sexual assault, such complaints are rare, and concern about them is vastly overblown in the public imagination.[25] The assumption that women who "cry rape" must be lying is nothing but a common sexist prejudice. Survivors want the scales of justice to be balanced by their own presumption of innocence.

Trauma survivors are at a further disadvantage in court because they often have difficulty telling their stories in a coherent manner, especially under hostile questioning. This is because traumatic memories are not like ordinary memories.[26] At the moment of impact, people often enter a numbed state of consciousness, technically called dissociation. The experience feels unreal; time may feel slowed down, and people may have the sense of leaving their bodies. Memories laid down in this altered state are fragmentary; they lack the logic of an ordinary narrative. Survivors may have intense and painful flashback recall of sensory details like smells and sounds but little or no recall of orienting details like time and place. There may be periods of partial or even complete amnesia. These well-documented disturbances of memory have been the source of much confusion. They often cause survivors to doubt themselves or fear they are losing their minds. Memory deficits have also been used frequently to attack survivors' credibility. In fact, such disturbances are completely consistent with a truthful account of a traumatic event.[27]

Many common prejudices about sexual assault were on display in 2018 when the US Senate conducted confirmation hearings for Brett Kavanaugh, an appellate court judge who had been nominated for the country's Supreme Court. In these hearings, psychology professor Christine Blasey Ford testified that the nominee and his friend had attempted to rape her years earlier when they were teenagers at an unsupervised party. Doubt was cast on her testimony because she could not give an exact date for the incident or name the location of the party. What she remembered most clearly, she said, was the *laughter* of her drunken assailants. That one word captured the humiliation of knowing that it was *fun* for these boys to pin her to a bed, cover her mouth, and make her fear for her life.

In voting to confirm Judge Kavanaugh, one senator explained that she found Dr. Ford's testimony perfectly credible but nevertheless thought that the nominee was entitled to the "presumption of innocence." Her statement reveals a common misunderstanding of law, and surely a senator, who is responsible for enacting laws, should know better. The presumption of innocence applies only in *criminal trials*. Judge Kavanaugh was not a criminal defendant in a court of law. His liberty was not at stake. A judgment as to his fitness for promotion to the country's highest court should have rested on a thorough and impartial investigation. Both those who supported the nominee and those who testified to his unfitness deserved to be heard with equal respect and without prejudice.

This did not happen. Following the successful playbook of his predecessor, Justice Clarence Thomas (who, when accused of sexual harassment, famously compared his Senate hearing to a "high-tech lynching"), Judge Kavanaugh subjected the senators to a furious, spitting performance of DARVO, an acronym coined by psychologist Jennifer Freyd that stands for "Deny, Attack, Reverse Victim and Offender." Apparently, no one screams as loudly as people who are facing the prospect of losing undeserved privileges. Intimidated by this display of rage from the nominee and his powerful supporters, including the president, the Senate abandoned further inquiry and hastily approved his nomination. The irony of having two credibly accused perpetrators of sexual misconduct sitting on the Supreme Court has not been lost on survivors. One might consider these two justices as the living embodiment of patriarchal impunity.

The Private Misfortunes of Two Girls

In the triangle of victim, perpetrator, and bystanders, impunity means in effect that the bystanders take the side of the perpetrator, and the weight of society and law condemns the victim to isolation. The crime alienates the victim not only from the person who violated her but also from all those who doubt her veracity, who blame her rather than the perpetrator, or who choose to turn a blind eye. Faced with the entrenched power of patriarchy, the moral community most commonly fails to come to the aid of the victim, leaving her alone to recover from her "private misfortune" as best she can. This is how tyranny is perpetuated.

In *Fortunate Daughter: A Memoir of Reconciliation*, writer Rosie McMahan, who grew up in Somerville, Massachusetts, a white, working-class town outside Boston, describes what betrayal by the moral community feels like to a kid who is both victim and witness under the tyranny of an abusive father. She describes her father, a "long-legged, burly man who worked long hours as a union member truck driver," as a complicated person who sometimes took her and her sisters on wonderful outdoor adventures to introduce his city girls to nature, but who at other times, especially when drinking, could be very violent, sparing no one in the family, not even their severely disabled brother. He also singled her out for sexual abuse and for favoritism that made her mother and sisters resent her. He regularly barked out orders, expecting to be obeyed without question, while the family lived in dread of his attacks and constantly placated him.

Rosie feels betrayed first of all by her mother: "I wished Mom would just stand up to him. I loathed her for so many things, including letting him tell her what to do and how to do it all the time." The second level of betrayal is institutional. Rosie describes an incident when she dials 911 (not for the first time). Her father is beating her younger sister, who has had the temerity to talk back to him. "Someone is going to get killed at my house if you don't send the police over right now," she pleads, realizing as she says it that this is indeed what she fears. Two officers from the Somerville police arrive. Rosie, from a hiding place under the porch, watches them enter the house and is impressed with their insignia of civic authority. She imagines how much more confident she would feel if she "held a weapon in [her] hand, wore a badge, walked in heavy-soled shoes."

However, the officers refuse to make an arrest, even when they see all the blood on her sister's face. Instead, they have a friendly, man-to-man chat with her father, after which one officer admonishes the girls, "We're gonna let your Daddy stay under one condition. You children must mind him better. Do what he tells you the first time he tells you." Rosie, who has come out from her hiding place, protests that the policeman doesn't understand. "My dad gets this way no matter what we do." "Now young lady," the officer scolds, "it's that kind of attitude that got you and your family into this mess in the first place." As they leave, she feels the helpless outrage of the powerless. "They should know better. They were supposed to protect us. They were the only ones Dad would obey, given that they had the law on their side. What did we have? We were just his little girls, Dad's property to do what he wanted with."[28]

This is how the institutions of the state have condoned and supported the rule of fathers for untold years. This is how children learn the rules of tyranny, lessons that are not soon forgotten.

For Black children, these lessons are compounded by a second interlocking tyranny: the deeply engrained legacy of centuries of enslavement and Jim Crow that we now call systemic racism. The lethal violence of the police against Black men and women is only the most obvious symptom of a repressive criminal justice system that routinely harasses and endangers Black people and disproportionately tracks them into prison.[29] In many Black communities, police are perceived more as an occupying army than as a source of protection. For abused women and children, this means that calling on the police for help would be unthinkable. Rosie McMahan was shocked to discover that the police sided with her father and blamed her and her sisters for provoking his violence. Many Black girls would not be shocked; they would be afraid to call the police in the first place.

Writer and documentary filmmaker Aishah Shahida Simmons recently put together an anthology of testimonies by Black women about sexual violence in Black families and communities, titled *Love WITH Accountability*. The book begins with her own testimony, in which she describes her childhood experience of sexual abuse by her grandfather. Her parents are both professionals with demanding careers in the cause of civil rights and human rights. Their work involves lots of travel, and they count on Aishah's paternal grandparents to take care of her when they are away. Aishah loves her "Pop Pop," but she hates what he does to her body when he sneaks into her bedroom at night. She describes her feelings for him as "one big painful conundrum."

Like Rosie McMahan, Aishah feels betrayed first of all by her mother. When she discloses what her grandfather is doing, her mother at first refuses to believe her. Aishah persists, with many tears. Finally convinced that Aishah must be telling the truth, her mother tells her ex-husband, Aishah's father, who says he will take care of the problem by speaking privately to his stepfather. No other intervention takes place, the parents assume that the problem is solved and continue to travel, and the abuse continues. Aishah's mother warns her that she must never tell her grandmother, because "this would kill her."

This warning puts Aishah in a position of imaginary power and responsibility, when in fact both power and responsibility belong to the perpetrator. The warning also places a barrier of silence between her and her beloved grandmother, thereby ensuring that her grandmother will never be a source of protection. For years, as she grows up, she is expected to act as though nothing has happened when she visits her grandparents for birthdays and holidays. She reflects, "I'm stunned by the mental acrobatics that I performed over three decades for the sake of maintaining family loyalty," and wonders, "What if my parents had held him accountable?"

Her mother, Dr. Gwendolyn Zoharah Simmons, writing the next chapter in the same anthology, struggles to come to grips with the fact that she never intervened to protect her child. She confesses that, without admitting it to herself, she had rationalized that her work for social justice was more important than anything else, even her daughter's safety. This was a lesson she had learned early on in the Black freedom movement, when, as a civil rights worker, she had to fight off one of her "comrades" who attempted to rape her. She never considered going to the police, but she did report him to the leadership of their organization, the Student Nonviolent Coordinating Committee. The leaders dismissed her complaint as *trivial* and chastised her for even bringing it up at a time when they were all about to risk their lives to register Black voters in the Deep South and challenge the tyranny of the Ku Klux Klan. The problem, as they saw it, was not that one of her "brothers" in the movement had tried to rape her but that she had resisted, and they ended by telling her simply, "You should have given him some."

Thus did Dr. Simmons learn the lessons of male entitlement: the timeless rules of patriarchy. Though she equaled her "brothers" in courage and shared their dangers, her body was still to be at their disposal. Sadly, as has often happened in liberation movements, the fight to overcome one form of tyranny demanded submission to another. These are the rules that she had internalized only too well when, years later, she betrayed her daughter.

Gwendolyn Simmons's remorseful public confession of her complicity is a model for the kind of acknowledgment, apology, and amends from bystanders that so many survivors long for. She admits to her selfishness in wanting Aishah to "forget about it, not to upset the happy family." She admits that she did not understand the tremendous harm she was inflicting on her daughter. She admits that she is shocked by and ashamed of her years of inaction. She grieves over the harm she has caused and is grateful to her daughter for persisting, even in anger, to demand accountability rather than breaking off relations entirely. In conclusion, she writes, "I can only pray that she forgives me and that I continue to learn from her example." Aishah, in turn, expresses gratitude to her mother for sharing her story and holding herself publicly accountable.[30]

Collectively, the women who contributed to *Love WITH Accountability* envision a kind of justice that centers on the needs of survivors and on healing the damaged relationship between survivors and their families and communities. They also seek a way to set firm limits on offenders' behavior without incarcerating them or treating them as monsters. Though most wish for an alternative to what they call the "criminal *in*justice system," they understand that such an alternative remains in the realm of aspiration, and they call on their wider moral community to help create it.

In Part Two of this book, we will listen in more depth to the voices of survivors as they lead us toward a better vision of justice, one that seeks to put an end to patriarchal impunity and to extend the healing principles of respect and fairness to everyone, even to people who have been traditionally subordinated and scorned.

PART TWO

VISIONS OF JUSTICE

4

ACKNOWLEDGMENT

Survivors tell us what they want. We should listen.[1]

—Alexandra Brodsky, *Sexual Justice*

The first precept of survivors' justice is the desire for community acknowledgment that a wrong has been done. This makes intuitive sense. If secrecy and denial are the tyrant's first line of defense, then public truth telling must be the first act of a survivor's resistance, and recognizing the survivor's claim to justice must be the moral community's first act of solidarity.

The First Speakout on Rape, organized by New York Radical Feminists, took place in 1971. There, the public testimony of survivors created a new kind of open courtroom, one in which violence against women would no longer be considered a *private misfortune* but rather viewed as a criminal injustice that had long been invisible and tacitly condoned. In declaring their stories with righteous outrage rather than shame, survivors collectively challenged the wider community to recognize truths long hidden. Fifty years later, when survivors organize, this remains their first demand. In 2020, Nikita Mitchell from Me Too International welcomed some twelve thousand survivors to an online meeting with these words: "Survivors across the country, across the globe have stepped into naming that 'I, too, have experienced sexual violence,' and 'I, too, deserve justice,' 'I, too, deserve to live in full dignity and humanity.'"

In this and the following chapters, we will hear the voices of the survivors who so generously shared their testimony with me. In our interviews, I asked them to imagine what justice might look like if they had complete freedom to determine what should be done. What would they wish for from the wider community? What would they wish for from offenders? Not surprisingly, the responses were quite varied, and yet, common themes emerged in their visions of justice: the need first of all for full acknowledgment and then for repair of the harm through apology and accountability. These are the themes that Part Two will elaborate.

The survivors whom I interviewed about their dreams of justice were in unanimous agreement on this first point: *They wanted the truth to be known.* One survivor of many years of domestic violence (identified only by her initials, ER) said simply, "I just want people to know who he is, what he did to me. This is what he did to another human being!" She also wanted him to face what he had done. "He would say that it's a lie, and he would believe it. He won't let himself know what he did. Sit down! You have to hear what you did!"

Many other survivors also felt it necessary to insist first and foremost on simple recognition of their humanity. Kate Price, a scholar in women's studies who is a survivor of incest and sex trafficking as a child, described what she thought should happen to the men who paid to use her body: "The sex buyers were truckers. They felt it was a woman's job to serve them. I want nothing to do with them. I would never want to see them—they make my skin crawl. But I would want them to hear my words: 'I'm a living, breathing human being. I'm not just a body.'" She, too, wanted her abusers to have to sit down and listen, and she wanted them to acknowledge publicly what they had done. "I would want them to hear from all the other children they've hurt. I would want their families to know, too. Maybe the men would be required to write a letter to their families and tell the truth." Daylight, in her mind, was the first step toward justice.

Many survivors sought acknowledgment of the truth not only from the perpetrators but also from the bystanders who were actively or passively complicit, and sometimes this kind of acknowledgment felt as important as the perpetrator's confession, or even more important. Dr. Price, for example, wanted the truth about sex trafficking of children and adolescents to be known in the wider community in the rust belt of Pennsylvania, where she had grown up. "Our culture fuels this," she said. "We breed this. In Appalachian culture you're supposed to be poor and know your place and like it. There's a pattern of exploitation." She didn't see the point of punishing the men who paid to use her body (though she did want her father, who sold her, to be punished), even though they must have known she was underage and drugged into passivity. "Even if we locked up every purchaser tomorrow there'd be another generation," she said. "So we need acknowledgment on a massive scale. We need the authority of the state creating a tribunal where victims' testimony was important."

Acknowledgment on a massive scale means recognition not only of the crimes committed by individual perpetrators but also of the complicity of all the people who enabled them. For instance, in 2003, soon after the *Boston Globe*'s Spotlight investigation first revealed numerous instances of child sexual abuse within the Catholic Church, a group of survivors came together to write a detailed manifesto titled "A Call to Reform the Archdiocese of Boston." Their very first request was for the church hierarchy to "admit to their culpability and guilt in knowingly moving pedophile priests from parish to parish, resulting in the additional abuse of countless children." They requested further that this acknowledgment be given publicly and in writing, and they wanted the church to stipulate "that the abuse was not the fault of the victims, and that the shame belongs only to those who did the abuse and those who covered it up."[2] Like my informants, these survivors, too, wanted all those implicated to admit how deeply these abuses of power were embedded in their traditional institutions. (We will learn more about what happened to this call to reform in Chapter 6.)

Beyond the acknowledgment of bare facts, survivors also wished for acknowledgment of harm. Though denial of the facts tends to be the perpetrator's first line of defense, when confronted with evidence, some will acknowledge the facts while dismissing or minimizing their importance. This is the "no big deal" defense: Why is she making such a fuss? Why is she being such a prude? She has no sense of humor. It's really just a *misunderstanding*. Besides, it's over. Why is she still bringing this up now? It's time for everyone to move on. Some perpetrators seem perfectly willing to admit what they have done but are either unaware or unconcerned that their victims were hurt and blame the victims for complaining.

"Rose," now a professor of criminal justice, tells of having been raped years ago, when she was a college student. She had been drinking at a party and must have passed out, because initially she had no memory of the incident. Word got around, and she first learned what had happened from a former boyfriend, who was upset with her for having "slept with" the boy who raped her. "I didn't even name this as rape for years," she admitted, with some bewilderment. The perpetrator was someone she knew from high school. "I didn't think he was a horrible person," she said. So she called him up to confront him. To her amazement, he didn't deny it. Instead, he was strangely matter-of-fact, saying, "Oh yeah, you were really out of it." "Not apologetic at all," she reported.

The offender was not alone in his lack of sympathy for her. The day after the rape, she went for medical attention because she was in pain and was found to have a bladder infection. "Must have been a rough night," the doctor said, with a smirk. "Like, 'this is what you get,'" Rose remarked.

Survivors do not want their injuries to be trivialized or ridiculed, and they do not want to be blamed for them. They do not want to be dismissed as overly emotional or told to "get over it." They want their communities to recognize and respect their suffering and to acknowledge the seriousness of the harm they have endured. As individuals they want the people who form their moral communities to hear them, to believe them, to recognize that they have been hurt, and to offer help and support. As a group, they want the larger public to recognize that survivors are everywhere and that sexual violence is a major public health problem, not simply a private misfortune.

For example, consider the story of Lybia Rivera, who came to Harvard University in 2003 from Puerto Rico, where she had grown up, to be a graduate student in Latin American studies. She described her childhood as quite privileged but also shaped by a "harsh Catholic environment where a woman is either a Madonna or a whore." She went to a private parochial school, sang in the church choir, and at one time even dreamed of being a nun. When she reached adolescence, her father pointed a gun at her and told her he would kill her if she did anything to damage the "family honor." In the meantime, however, she had already silently suffered years of sexual abuse by a prominent, respected neighbor, a member of the elite of her small town, so she already felt permanently dishonored. Her refuge was the library in her home, where she developed her intellectual interests. When she came to the university, she hoped to escape the stifling culture of her childhood, and she planned to work on a project to deepen democracy in Latin America.

Rivera went to work for a professor, Jorge Dominguez, who was one of the most distinguished faculty members in her field. Unbeknownst to her, he was also notorious for sexually harassing students and employees, having already been disciplined once by the university, in 1983. Nevertheless, he had been steadily promoted, and by the time Rivera arrived, he had been named director of the Center for International Affairs. "When men see themselves in power they think that they deserve everything," she reflected. "Some people thrive on abusing women, and they are very good at detecting vulnerability." The professor fantasized openly about how much he would enjoy raping her. Other members of his staff told her that "whatever he wanted he would get."

This hostile climate inflamed Rivera's long-standing posttraumatic stress disorder. She was able to do well in her courses but feared that she could not complete her dissertation on time. When she went to the university's disability office to ask for an extension because of the problems she was having with her professor, she was told that obviously she was "not Harvard material." This judgment reflected not only the implicit racism and sexism of the institution but also the cover it gave to a notorious predator by failing to acknowledge the impact of his behavior and instead shaming and ostracizing his victim. "I did have good grades," she reflected, "and I didn't want people to say 'Poor Lybia,' but someone like me would need a little extra consideration." She never finished her dissertation and eventually left the university.

Years later, in 2018, the *Chronicle of Higher Education* published an article in which eighteen women publicly accused Dominguez of sexual harassment. The complaints covered a period of over thirty-five years; the earliest known instance was in 1979, the most recent in 2015. Dominguez denied the allegations, suggesting that his behavior may have been "misinterpreted" (in other words, it was all a *misunderstanding*), but he nonetheless found it prudent to take early retirement.

In 2019, after an investigation, the university found the allegations to be credible, stripped the professor of his emeritus status and privileges, and disinvited him from campus. In 2021, the president of the university publicly apologized to the first woman who had come forward and "to those whose subsequent sexual harassment might have been avoided if Harvard had taken timely and appropriate action."[3] But as of this date, beyond official apology, the focus of the university's actions has been belated punishment of the offender and formation of committees to make recommendations for the future. This may be cold comfort to those women whose careers were derailed over more than three decades. There has been no indication that Harvard might recognize any responsibility to repair the harms that were done.

Rivera has moved on with her life. She married a fellow graduate student, who has been supportive and understanding in a way that her family of origin was not. "He was healthy, so I had to get healthy," she said. She has never given up her intellectual pursuits, having tattooed on her wrist two Chinese characters, meaning "pursue knowledge and philosophy." She hopes by her testimony to contribute to the growing public understanding of the difficulty of being a student with PTSD. Like so many survivors, she has made meaning of her story by making it a gift to others, hoping to heal not only herself but also other survivors and even, perhaps, to bend a complicit institution toward justice.

Vindication

Survivors wish for many kinds of reparative action from their communities, ranging from immediate help and support in a crisis, as Rivera requested, to broad educational programs for prevention of violence. Prior to any form of action, however, survivors wish for moral vindication. They want bystanders to take a stand, recognize that a wrong has been done, and un-ambiguously denounce the crime. In the face of common prej-udices that blame survivors for whatever happened to them, they want assurances from the community that they did not de-serve to be abused. They want the burden of shame lifted from their shoulders and placed on the shoulders of the perpetrators, where it belongs. This is the consensus that emerged from my interviews. The people I spoke with were keenly aware that the crimes were intended to dishonor and isolate them; they sought, therefore, the restoration of their own honor and the reestab-lishment of their own connections with the community. They were unanimous in defining justice as both acknowledgment and vindication.

Our justice system, however, makes both acknowledgment and vindication difficult to achieve. The story of Ross Cheit, an attorney and a professor of political science who is also a survi-vor of sexual abuse in childhood, illustrates both what it feels like to gain acknowledgment and vindication and what an enor-mous battle is often required to gain even these first conditions of justice. As an adult, Cheit recalled that he had been abused by the director of a summer camp run by the San Francisco Boys' Choir, a revered institution where he grew up. He made inquiries and discovered that many other boys had also been abused at the choir's summer camp. He and two other survi-vors filed criminal complaints, but it turned out that no charges could be brought because the statute of limitations had expired.

Instead, Cheit initiated civil lawsuits for damages against both the perpetrator, a man named Bill Farmer, and the choir.

Theoretically, civil suits offer survivors a less forbidding avenue for justice than criminal complaints. Civil law is about disputes between two citizens or between an individual and an organization. The state, in the person of the judge, is the arbiter of the dispute, but it does not represent either party, as it does in criminal law. The survivor has the choice to initiate a complaint. If a claim of harm is filed, the accused is required to respond, and the court is obliged to hear both sides and to sign off on its resolution. If the harm is proved, the remedy is money, and the seriousness of the harm can be judged by the amount of monetary damages the offender is required to pay in restitution.

Because the liberty of the accused is not at stake in civil law, the scales are not weighted in the defendant's favor, as they are in criminal trials. Though the burden of proof is still on the complainant, there is no presumption of innocence. Because both plaintiff and defendant enter the court as equal citizens before the law, the scales of justice are theoretically balanced. Moreover, the standard of proof is simply the "preponderance of evidence," not the more rigorous "beyond a reasonable doubt" standard.

One might think that these distinctions would make civil trials a more accessible form of justice for survivors. In fact, however, civil lawsuits are still an ordeal. They still take place within an adversarial system, where survivors can expect to be subjected to all sorts of invasive attempts to dig up dirt about them, including subpoenas for mental health records, as well as shaming and ugly personal attacks in court.

Lawsuits also require legal representation, and that can be very expensive. Survivors often find themselves outmatched. For example, according to attorney and feminist advocate Alexandra Brodsky, who is just five years out of law school, widely recognized professional guidelines suggest that she would be expected to charge nearly $500 an hour.[4] Citizens may be equal before the law in theory, but in practice, when members of a subordinated group seek justice in court, the disparities in power between plaintiff and defendant are all too apparent.

Ross Cheit, a middle-aged, married, heterosexual white man, recognizes all the privileges of gender, education, race, and class that gave him status and credibility. "The first time I talked to a lawyer, he says to me 'Of course you'll be believed, because you're a man! Women are going in with people thinking you'd lie. Men: God, why would you lie about *that*!'" He also understood how the adversarial system worked and could say to the opposing counsel, "If you want hardball, I'll play hardball. I know I'll win." His wife remarked that she thought civil lawsuits were designed for men.

Because the defendant, Bill Farmer, failed to appear in court on the appointed day, the case was automatically adjudicated in Cheit's favor. A separate hearing was held, nevertheless, in order for the judge to determine the amount of damages. For Cheit, even with his legal background, testifying in court was a very intense and emotional experience that brought him to tears. "I went on the stand and told what happened," he reported. "The judge put a dollar value of half a million dollars on my claim. For money I'd never thought I would see, never will see, I remember the feeling was overwhelming. Not only did the judge believe me, but he also thought this was important! The idea of money does mean something. That was the day the system acknowledged the damage to me, valued me. They could have said 'Why are you still talking about this now,' but they didn't."

Cheit's parents accompanied him to court when he testified and also signed statements of support in his lawsuit against the choir, arguing that the institution they trusted had betrayed them as well as their son. "It meant a lot to me," he reflected. "The notion that they would do that, standing with me, saying the injury isn't just to one, it affects others as well." In adding their voices to his claim, his parents exemplified the basic principle of a moral community, that injury to one is an injury to all. This starts with the family, of course, but hopefully extends beyond it.

Cheit was not satisfied with a judgment that acknowledged harm to him alone. When he reached out to other alumni of the summer camp, he found many who acknowledged that they had been abused but very few who were willing to testify in public. He was gratified to find two men who did come forward as corroborating witnesses during the initial criminal investigation, before the courts determined that it was too late to bring charges. For civil lawsuits, however, the justice system generally structures the harm as an individual rather than an institutional problem, and so there is no shared remedy for institutional betrayals. There is such a thing as a class-action suit, and we will hear about some of them in later chapters, but there are many restrictions on who can qualify for such a remedy. "I knew the chorus had covered it up," he said, "and I had this naïve view that a lawsuit could have made that change. I wanted them to send a letter to everyone who had gone to that camp. It was absolutely the right thing to do." But the choir's attorney was adamantly opposed to the idea. "You can't make us do that," the defense attorney said. "That's not a remedy to your claim. What do *you* want?"

After grueling and protracted litigation that he described as "a fight to the bitter end," the chorus eventually settled Cheit's suit out of court. This is the way most civil cases are resolved, in a war of nerves that sometimes drags out until the morning the trial is scheduled to begin. Usually such settlements are made by payment of a sum of money with no admission of responsibility, often with nondisclosure agreements (NDAs). The chorus's high-powered attorney was baffled, because Cheit obviously didn't care about how much money was offered, even though he knew that, unlike the abuser, the chorus would actually pay the damages. Instead, he refused to sign an NDA and insisted on a public admission of responsibility for harboring a predator as a nonnegotiable condition of the settlement. "They didn't understand the psychological meaning," he explained. "Acknowledgment is a balm."

By pursuing justice in civil court and fighting to the bitter end, Cheit was able to achieve the first goal of survivor justice. He gained validation from the court when the perpetrator defaulted, and he also was able to obtain a grudging public acknowledgment of both the facts and the harm from the complicit institution. Some of his friends and legal colleagues were amazed, because the settlement even included an admission that the institution's conduct was wrong and a pro forma apology. "Lawyers don't *do* this," they exclaimed. But his story also shows how incredibly difficult it was to achieve these first objectives, even with all the legal expertise, social support, financial resources, and determination that Cheit could muster. The fact that so many cases of this kind are settled with nondisclosure agreements reveals the lengths to which offenders and their enabling institutions will go to buy silence and the way the justice system in turn enables them to do so.

Cheit was proud of what he had achieved but remains dissatisfied with the justice system because he was unable to gain what many survivors want beyond acknowledgment and vindication: a genuine apology, accountability for the guilty parties, with prevention of future harm, and a sincere effort to make amends to all those who were harmed. Years later, Cheit heard through the grapevine that Bill Farmer had moved to Texas and was starting a boys' church choir there. The law offered no mechanism to prevent this and no way to compel the San Francisco Boys' Choir to reach out to all the other men who might have been abused years before at the summer camp. As for the formal apology, Cheit had this to say: "It was *called* an apology, and as a lawyer I understood what it was. There were negotiations about the words, like 'If you were damaged.' What do you mean, *if*? In the end, the most important thing was that they didn't deny it."

This case illustrates how hard survivors have to fight to gain even their first objective: public acknowledgment of the truth. It does offer hope that with courage and tenacity, survivors can sometimes prevail in the existing justice system, but only rarely, and then only to a limited extent. Acknowledgment and vindication are necessary but not sufficient conditions for realizing survivors' visions of justice, because these visions extend beyond acknowledgment to include apology, accountability, and amends. We turn now to the question of apology.

5

APOLOGY

Apologies don't count from the pulpit. They don't count from a spokesperson. They don't count from a press release. They only count in person. I learned that in first grade, from Sister Mary Adele.

—Stephen Rubino, an attorney for survivors
of childhood abuse by Catholic clergy[1]

Many survivors yearn for a genuine apology. They want the perpetrators to admit their crimes and take full responsibility, with remorse and without excuses, to recognize the suffering they have caused, and to show that they are willing to do whatever needs to be done to make amends. True apology also offers a promise, implicit or explicit, that the offender has undergone a moral awakening: that he is a changed man and will never repeat his crime. Genuine apologies are personal, they are emotional, and they create the possibility of repairing a relationship.

When the offender humbles himself to beg for pardon, the gesture represents a reversal of the power dynamic between victim and offender. The power to grant or withhold pardon belongs to the victim. Such gestures of humility go a long way to restoring the victim's dignity and self-respect.[2] They assuage feelings of helpless rage and bitterness that torment the victim, and often they call forth spontaneous feelings of forgiveness.[3] Unfortunately, such full and genuine apologies are rare.

In *Fortunate Daughter: A Memoir of Reconciliation*, Rosie Mc-Mahan, whom we met in Chapter 3, tells a story of apology and forgiveness that led to restored family relationships after years of domestic violence and sexual abuse. The story is inspirational but also instructive. More than a decade of work in recovery preceded this outcome, and achieving it required a great deal of social support for all members of the family.

Rosie's recovery began at age twelve with the first step out of isolation, when her mother and sisters found their way to Al-Anon, the self-help group for family members of people with alcoholism. In many ways, this was the beginning of a new moral community, an antidote to the tyranny of the father. Al-Anon meetings are free and readily available in local church basements in many communities throughout the country and in many countries throughout the world. The meetings are governed by the Twelve Traditions, which keep meetings confidential and democratic and prevent them from being hijacked by charismatic or domineering leaders. Members of Al-Anon practice the Twelve Steps themselves, beginning by acknowledging their powerlessness over the person with alcoholism. With this acknowledgment comes the understanding that they are not to blame for what he does ("Didn't cause it, can't cure it, can't control it") and that they must focus on their own self-care rather than trying to placate or rescue the drinker ("Let go and let God").

Through acquaintances at Al-Anon, Rosie found her way to a therapist she calls "Ella," who worked at a free storefront clinic in Somerville run by a collective of radical feminists. She described Ella as the first person who helped her and her sisters. Ella's colleague, a psychiatrist whom she refers to in the book as "Dr. Yaffe," began working with Rosie's mother. With the support of therapy and a sponsor from Al-Anon, Rosie's mother finally made the decision to flee with the children to a battered women's shelter recently opened by community activists. After several failed attempts, she also finally obtained a court order that compelled Rosie's father to leave the home and stay away from the family.

This was the only point in the story in which the formal institutions of justice intervened in any helpful way. Mostly, help for Rosie and her family came from the women's liberation movement. The legal reforms that gave abused women the right to seek civil restraining orders in court and the organizing efforts that created battered women's shelters and women's clinics were among the signal accomplishments of Second Wave feminism in the 1970s. In other words, without a feminist resistance movement, there was simply no recourse for these girls or their mother against the power of patriarchy.

Though stopping the violence was a major turning point for the family, recovery still took many more years. Rosie's mother ended therapy once she and her husband separated, but Rosie remained in therapy with Ella off and on, through a troubled adolescence and a period of estrangement from the family. Eventually she managed to work her way through college. She and her two sisters graduated at the same time, a first for this working-class family. Her mother hosted a big celebration, attended by many relatives, but not by her father. Ella stopped by to offer her congratulations.

Then came another turning point: after many periods of sobriety and relapses, and after many separations and attempts to reconcile with his wife, Rosie's father had a heart attack that almost killed him. Rosie, her mother, and her sisters loyally rallied to keep vigil at his bedside while he was in intensive care, and when he was able to communicate once more, he expressed his gratitude. He survived. Given a second chance at life, he finally made a commitment to sobriety and agreed to engage in sex offender treatment offered by a program for batterers.

Only then, at age twenty-six, was Rosie ready to confront her parents. She invited them to meet with her in Ella's office. She worked for a long time with Ella to prepare an impact statement she wanted to read to them. Dr. Yaffe, for her part, reached out to the parents to help them prepare. She explained that they would be asked to listen without interruption, and they agreed to attend the session together.

As if in an alternative courtroom of her own choosing, Rosie began her testimony, addressing her father:

> You made me hate my body.
> You made me scared of myself.
> You made me think that men weren't human.

You would yell at me.
You would slap me.
You would strap me.
You tried to possess me.
You tried to own me.

Rosie continued speaking about the impact of her father's abuse. When she finished her testimony, both parents were sobbing. Ella invited them to respond. Rosie's father said, "I know I did these things. I can't take that away. I'm sorry." He added that he understood there was no excuse for what he did. Her mother added, "I knew it would carry on into her life. I knew it would make her life harder. I wish I could take it away, I really do." Rosie felt the sincerity of these apologies, and for the moment, that's all she needed. She felt uplifted, "free of gravity," as Ella congratulated them, saying that she was proud of them all.

The reconciliation that followed proved durable enough that in later years, when the three sisters were partnered and raising children of their own, the three generations of the family could gather safely, and Rosie's parents could have loving relationships with their grandchildren, though, by agreement, the children were never left alone with them. In publishing her memoir, Rosie writes, "I want this story to become part of the solution, adding to the national dialogue on how to 'restore justice' in a family riddled with childhood abuse and sexual trauma."[4]

I have quoted at length from Rosie's story to illustrate what a genuine apology looks like. The words don't matter nearly as much as the emotion that is shared. To Rosie, the true expressions of remorse were found in her parents' tears. They were crying, not because they were sorry for themselves but because they were sorry for what they had done to her. In an interview following the publication of her book, she added, "There's something really powerful about having your perpetrators be fully remorseful again and again. It's how they lived the rest of their lives."[5]

The reader may have already guessed that I am "Dr. Yaffe." "Ella" is my old friend and closest colleague Emily Schatzow, who was trained in family therapy and has worked with many incest survivors on family disclosures. (We reveal our identities at Rosie's initiative and with her permission.) I tell this story in part because it is so terribly rare. No matter how passionately survivors may wish for an apology, they must be fully prepared for disappointment, since they are more likely to meet with denial, excuses, or blame than with acknowledgment and repentance. For this reason, we advise survivors not to proceed with a face-to-face encounter unless they feel sure that the success of the meeting will not be contingent on the perpetrator's response. The main purpose of the meeting is simply for the survivor to speak her truth and to put the perpetrator on notice that his victim will no longer be silenced.[6]

The rare heartfelt apology, when it happens, can be truly uplifting. But while genuine apologies foster the hope that evil deeds can be redeemed, insincere apologies add insult to injury by mocking that hope. For this reason, while all the survivors I interviewed agreed emphatically about their desire for acknowledgment and vindication, they were ambivalent about wanting an apology. Many feared that any expressions of regret would simply be another form of manipulation. They doubted whether their abusers were capable of empathy or whether they could trust any expression of remorse from their abusers. No one wanted the infamous "politician's apology," always offered in the passive voice or in the conditional: "Mistakes were made," or "We regret *if* anyone was offended."

Many perpetrators are not, in fact, truly sorry for what they have done. Professor Ross Cheit, whom we met in Chapter 4, spent many years as a prison volunteer working with sex offenders as part of his survivor mission. He taught ethics classes and observed their therapy groups. He came away with this impression: "The guys I see are the best of the bunch. They've admitted their crime, and they're in a treatment program. But I'm really struck, watching them struggle: They're incapable of putting themselves in others' shoes. They don't get the consequences. They know it's wrong, and they're sorry, really sorry—because they're in prison."

Few of the survivors who spoke with me had ever actually sought an apology from any of the people who abused them, and even fewer had received one. In addition to distrusting the perpetrator, some were clear that they did not want the sort of reconciliation that might be expected to follow an apology. "Caroline," a poet and incest survivor, explained why she never wished for an apology from the older brother who abused her: "I suspect he would *enjoy* talking about what he did. He wouldn't really be sorry, in the sense of remorse or regret. I would feel slimed all over again. And I would be wary of an apology, because then I would feel pressure to forgive him."

Forgiveness?

This brings us to the complicated question of forgiveness. The modern movement for restorative justice (discussed in greater depth in the next chapter) envisions healing the harms of crime through a face-to-face encounter between perpetrator and victim, witnessed by the community, in which the perpetrator's acknowledgment, apology, and promise to make amends are followed by forgiveness and reconciliation.[7] Is this indeed a better form of justice for survivors?

A bit of historical perspective may shed light on this question. Classical scholar David Konstan, in his thought-provoking 2010 book *Before Forgiveness: The Origins of a Moral Idea*,[8] maintains that the modern concept of *interpersonal* forgiveness is of relatively recent origin. It is not found in classical antiquity or even, surprisingly, in the Old or New Testament. In the Bible and in the works of Jewish and early Christian theologians, only *God* has both the authority and the grace to forgive. The common adage "To err is human, to forgive, divine" illustrates this idea. For many centuries Jewish and Christian theology understood that only God could see into the human heart and recognize true remorse and penitence, the necessary preconditions for forgiveness. Konstan argues further that the modern concept of interpersonal forgiveness is somewhat problematic because it is predicated on the notion that the offender has had a genuine change of heart. But how often does this actually happen, and how can mere humans tell with certainty the difference between true remorse and apologies that are transitory or merely transactional?

It may be for this reason that very few of the survivors who spoke with me actually desired a personal encounter of the sort envisioned by restorative justice, and several, like "Caroline," explicitly rejected the idea. Many survivors, rather than aspiring to heal their relationships with their abusers, simply wanted nothing to do with them. Mary Margaret Giannini, an attorney for the city of Jacksonville, Florida, and a rape survivor, explained how she felt about this matter when I first interviewed her in 2002. The man who assaulted her was a stranger who took advantage of her kindness and naïve trust by talking his way into her home, claiming that his truck had been stolen, and asking to make a phone call. The rapist was arrested, pled guilty, and was sentenced to prison.

Though an Episcopalian minister's daughter and an actively practicing Christian, Giannini said that for a long time she couldn't pray for the perpetrator. "When I think of the man who raped me," she said, "reconciliation—redemption—it's not an issue in my mind. Reconciliation: that will most likely never happen. I don't know that it needs to happen. He doesn't need my forgiveness. He needs his Creator's forgiveness. I have no control over that, thank Goodness! I don't want to be a part of his recovery process. I've had enough work to do on my own."

Of course, forgiveness means different things to different people. To some survivors, forgiveness means unilaterally letting go of rage and bitterness. It is not in any way contingent on the perpetrator's remorse or apology; rather, it is simply part of the survivor's own healing. In that sense of the word, many of my informants aspired to it. This kind of letting go cannot be achieved simply by an act of will, however. Emotionally, it is quite different from the immediate, spontaneous, and liberating feeling of forgiveness that many people experience in response to a genuine expression of remorse. To arrive at this unilateral type of forgiveness requires a period of active grieving for everything that has been lost and all the harms that cannot be repaired. Survivors sometimes describe this process as letting go of all their own self-blame and finally forgiving *themselves*, besides letting go of their anger at the perpetrator. As Mary Walsh, a survivor of domestic violence, put it, "Forgiveness is giving up all hope of a better past."

In 2020, almost two decades after her first interview with me, Giannini reflected again on her feelings about resentment and forgiveness. In the interim, the offender had died in prison, and she had attended his funeral, sitting quietly in the parking lot of the church so that she would not disturb his family with her presence. She was glad to know that he did have a family who cared about him. She wrote,

My words on the page from those years ago may read "harder" than I meant to convey. I think I was trying to suggest that—at least at that time—I didn't feel big enough (as in a god greater than ourselves) to take on the role of forgiveness, but that I hoped the man who raped me did have some sort of relationship with divinity, that he would seek wholeness there. Today? I think learning of [his] death shifted things . . . I realized that I was tired, emotionally tired, of directing angst, resentment, anger towards him. I was healthier and happier when I "let him go." I don't know if it is called forgiveness, but I would call it peace.

Many survivors concurred in their wish to "let go" of the perpetrator and all he represented in their minds. Some survivors described their persistent feelings of resentment and their fantasies of revenge almost as foreign bodies or toxic residues of the perpetrator's violence, and they longed to be rid of them. Amy Bradford, an artist and rape survivor, described a dream in which a dinosaur came and trampled on her rapist. In the dream she was gleeful; awake, she found the dream grotesque. The last thing she wanted in her life was more violence.

Interestingly, her husband, Bill Bradford, was much more comfortable feeling vengeful than she was. I have often found this to be true, that friends and family of survivors are much more vocal and much less conflicted about their desires for revenge than the survivors themselves. This is particularly true when survivors know their abusers well and can see something of their humanity. Bradford said he wished he had killed the rapist, whom he called an "evil force, not a human being." But even he was mollified when asked whether a real apology would make a difference. "I think that if I could put that rapist in a chair," he said, "I know this will never happen, but if he would admit it was a horrible thing, express regret, apologize to her and then do the same for me, I think that would help. I'm tired of being angry. Boy, I'm surprised to hear myself say that!"

Another rape survivor, Sarah Johnson, a nurse, said she wished she could make the boy who raped her at a high school party feel "the worst pain in the world." "I know people talk about forgiving," she said, "but I'm bitter. I will never be able to forgive him." A moment later, however, she added, "If he were to say, 'Sarah, I'm sorry and I need help,' I would say:

"Thank you, God!' Then I wouldn't hate him so." Once again, just the thought of an apology seemed to mollify vengeful feelings. Even in imagination, apparently, true apology carries some of its magic.

Playwright and feminist activist Eve Ensler, who has now renamed herself as V, has developed this magic to the fullest in her book *The Apology*. This is a monologue written in the voice of her father, who physically and sexually abused her in childhood. With the power of her creativity as a playwright, she invoked the spirit of her late father, who had never apologized to her in his lifetime.[9] In a recent talk, she described writing the apology as a practice of liberation, "transforming who he was in me." As a method, she listed four steps that must take place in the (imagined) mind of the perpetrator: first, engaging in deep introspection about what made him capable of his crimes; second, acknowledging in full detail what he had done; third, developing empathy: feeling and understanding the impact of the harms he had inflicted; and finally, taking full responsibility and making the apology. These steps are remarkably similar to those practiced in Twelve Step programs like Alcoholics Anonymous. The fourth step, "a searching and fearless moral inventory," leads in subsequent steps to acknowledgment, apology, and amends to all those whom the person has harmed.

After writing the book, V changed her name. Though writing the book was painful, when it was done, she felt released from her father's grip and no longer wanted to be identified by the patronymic. She ended the book with the words "Old man, be gone." With the power of her imagination, she had managed to create an "I and Thou" dialogue with a redeemed father with whom reconciliation was possible. "When it is offered and received," she concluded, "an authentic apology creates an alchemical, physical, psychological, spiritual dissolving of the offense in the body, of rancor and bitterness and the need for revenge and hate. This is actually what forgiveness feels like."[10]

V cautioned, however, that the victim should never be expected or pressured to forgive, even when the perpetrator does offer a sincere and full apology. My informants were in full agreement on this point. To the extent that they felt social pressure toward forgiveness, they tended to resent and resist it.

Resisting Forgiveness

Modern Christian religious teachings frequently exhort victims to transcend their anger through forgiveness rather than taking action against those who have offended them, and the virtues of forgiveness have always been especially recommended to women and to members of other subordinate groups, whose justified resentment might make those in power uncomfortable. The benefits of forgiveness have been promoted not only for the victim's soul but also for her sanity. An initiative by the Templeton Foundation, a private, Christian, nonprofit organization, proposed to document the effectiveness of so-called forgiveness therapy for victims of crime. One funded study described a program of weekly therapy for incest survivors organized around an explicit agenda of forgiveness.[11] Based on very limited data, the author claimed that learning forgiveness produced more positive results than any other known treatment for this population, a judgment not generally shared by most experts in the field of traumatic stress.

Survivors are justifiably suspicious of the idea of forgiving their assailants, especially in the absence of strong assurances of a true change of heart. In a sermon titled "The Thorny Question of Forgiveness," Anne Marie Hunter, a Protestant minister and a survivor of domestic violence, explained why she questioned the religious mandate to forgive: "The profound truth is this: it is wonderful and Christian to forgive. And, sometimes, it is the wrong thing to forgive. Because we know now that abusers are often contrite afterwards. They say they're sorry. They say they'll change. They say it will never happen again. But without the help of a state-certified batterer's treatment program, it *will* happen again."[12] Reverend Hunter knows all too well that apologies and expressions of remorse, even if apparently sincere in the moment, can be among the most effective methods that abusers employ to keep their victims under their control.

In her own survivor mission, Hunter works to educate clergy and religious congregations about the realities of domestic violence and to change the patriarchal doctrines and attitudes that align the church with abusers. She understands that her work challenges the basic structures of the Christian faith as it has been established for the last seventeen hundred years. "When you have a God who's judgmental and all-powerful and all-knowing, that sounds a lot like a batterer. Religious women who believe God is on the side of the batterer will say 'this is just my cross to bear.' The religious community's bias is to force forgiveness. They cry 'peace, peace,' when there is no peace."

Needless to say, Hunter's views are controversial within modern Christian theology. Did not Jesus exhort his followers to turn the other cheek? In answer, she quotes a domestic violence survivor who told her, "I turn the other cheek, and turn the other cheek, and now I have no face left." The problem, as Hunter sees it, is that exhorting victims to forgive their abusers is always so much easier than confronting the abusers and actually putting a stop to the violence. "I have yet to hear anyone say 'I am setting limits because I am a Christian,'" she says. "Rather than moving victims to forgiveness, we need to be thinking about moving perpetrators to contrition and changed behavior."

Though this may be a minority view, Hunter is not alone in her insistence that true repentance must precede forgiveness. An eminent member of the Catholic clergy, the archbishop of Dublin and primate of Ireland, has taken a similar stance. Expressing his dismay about the worldwide scourge of child sexual abuse by Catholic priests, the Most Reverend Diarmuid Martin reflected that in his experience, the lack of genuine remorse on the part of the offenders was "one of the greatest insults" for survivors, and he added, "It is very hard to speak of meaningful forgiveness of an offender when the offender refuses to recognize the full significance of the facts."[13]

Jewish religious teachings tracing back to the writings of the twelfth-century scholar Moses Maimonides accord with this position: forgiveness must be earned by the practice of *teshuvah*, or repentance. According to modern religious scholar Yerachmiel Gorelik, "The elements of teshuvah include rigorous self-examination and require the perpetrator to engage with the victim, by confessing, expressing regret and making every effort possible to right the wrong that he committed." Rabbi Gorelik adds that forgiveness without *teshuvah* is actually destructive to a moral community. "For while granting earned forgiveness is an act of grace that may be emotionally restorative, uplifting and inspiring, nevertheless, to grant unearned forgiveness is not kind but callous, and can only further desensitize both the perpetrator and the victim to distinctions of morality."[14]

In the view of these religious leaders, reconciliation should follow only after justice has been done. And justice means that the community has intervened to put a stop to the abuse and that the abuser acknowledges what he has done, takes full responsibility for his behavior, and shows his repentance by his willingness to do whatever is necessary to make amends. These leaders challenge us, the bystanders, to end our complicity, active or passive, with perpetrators of patriarchal violence and to undertake the serious and demanding task of holding them accountable. This is not something that survivors can do alone; nor should it be their sole responsibility. It is a task that requires a new kind of commitment from the moral community.

6

ACCOUNTABILITY

If no one's punishment leads to
My salvation, then accountability is what waits.

—Jericho Brown, "Inaugural"[1]

Acknowledgment of the survivor's truth, acknowledgment of the harm she has suffered, and full apology, with remorse and without excuses—for many survivors, these are the requisite actions by which perpetrators and bystanders can begin the process of healing, moving from truth to repair. In the traditional justice system, we would speak of the perpetrator's confession and guilty plea, and the consequences would be some form of punishment. But many survivors feel very ambivalent about punishment because it does nothing substantive to repair the harm that has been done to them. Rather, they try to envision alternatives that would require the perpetrator and complicit bystanders to make amends. What might it mean to hold perpetrators accountable for repairing the harm they have done? What might it mean to hold bystanders accountable for acts of complicity and collusion? What about acts of omission, indifference, or willful blindness? These are the questions that survivors grapple with as they try to define a new idea of justice.

Although survivors are so often stereotyped as vengeful and excessively punitive, most of those I interviewed seemed remarkably uninterested in punishment. Some were opposed to punishment on principle; others simply didn't see what good punishing the offender would do for them or for anyone else. In general, they wanted justice to be centered more on themselves than on the perpetrator, more on healing than on just deserts. As far as the perpetrator was concerned, they much preferred the idea of rehabilitation to punishment. According to a recent nationwide survey, crime victims in general share these views.[2] However, these priorities put them at complete odds with our current criminal justice system.

For punishment is the metric of justice in criminal law. As the agent of criminal justice, the state establishes uniform, quantifiable standards of punishment (i.e., fines, prison sentences) that are supposed to be applied equitably and rationally in proportion to the seriousness of the crime. This is considered a major strength of retributive justice: its aspiration to be standardized, proportional, and fair to all. In practice, as is well known, the system does not treat all citizens equitably, and it inflicts profoundly disparate punishments based on gender, race, and class.

The evolution of state-based criminal justice is commonly viewed as progress compared to premodern, private, or communitarian systems of redress. According to conventional wisdom, by assuming the initiative to establish the truth and punish transgressions, the state curbs the dangers of vigilantism, gang vendettas, and family blood feuds and sets limits on arbitrary, cruel, and excessive punishments. It also offers the possibility of justice to many victims who would otherwise be powerless to seek accountability in any form. When the state assumes the role of the injured party, however, crime victims are reduced to the status of peripheral actors in the high-conflict drama of prosecution versus defense and subjected to hostile interrogation and shaming when they testify as witnesses to their own experiences. As we have seen in previous chapters, the criminal justice system offers victim witnesses no effective protection from bullying and intimidation and very little opportunity to tell their stories on their own terms.

For survivors of gender-based violence and other subordinated groups, this means that agency is taken away from them twice, first when they are victimized and once again when they seek redress of harm. We saw in Chapter 2 how even such a modest reform as allowing victims to address the court in their own words with impact statements in the sentencing phase of trials has proved controversial. How much more radically would our justice system have to change to center on the well-being of the victim rather than the punishment of the offender?

Alexa Sardina, who is now a criminal justice professor, tells of being raped at knifepoint in her first week away from home when she was a college freshman. She is among that rare 1 to 5 percent of rape survivors to gain what is conventionally called justice in criminal court. The rapist, a stranger who broke into her dormitory, was arrested, tried, found guilty, and sentenced to a long prison term. Nevertheless, the process was an ordeal for her. She dropped out of school and went home to her parents. Each time she had to appear in court, she relived the trauma. The defense insinuated that she had invited the rapist into the dorm for sex. At one point during the trial, she ran away from the courthouse, crying, "I want to go home!" and had to be pursued and escorted back.

"Often I felt like a piece of evidence," she said. "It's not my case. It's not! You're objectified a second time." Her mother described the trial process as "one nightmare after another." From her perspective, it appeared that defendants had more rights than victims. The process was also very expensive for the family. Each time there was a hearing in court, they had to travel to upstate New York from their home several hours away. Though the family had expected that the conviction and sentencing of the offender would bring them "closure," when the trial was over, they felt no relief or satisfaction; in fact, they discovered that the long process of recovery had just barely begun.

Asked what would be a better form of justice, Sardina reflected, "There was no way for me to say to him 'Why did you do this?' or for him to acknowledge what he did and take responsibility. There was no opportunity for a personal exchange. We need more protection for survivors from being smeared, and we need more incentive for defendants to acknowledge rather than deny, deny, deny." She saw only too clearly how the existing system gave offenders every incentive to be steadfast in refusing to admit what they had done and instead to attack the credibility of their victims.

Many of the other survivors whom I interviewed expressed similar sentiments. The justice system offered them very little incentive to endure the rigors of a trial, since few sought satisfaction in the outcome that a conviction would provide: punishment of the offenders. Those who chose to participate in the criminal justice system did so mainly because they saw no other way to prevent the offenders from repeating their crimes.[3] Rather than wishing to make the offenders suffer for the sake of retribution, most survivors wanted the offenders to admit their crimes, to be exposed to public censure, to understand the harm that they had caused, to feel genuine remorse, and to be rehabilitated. The unanswered question was how to bring those changes about.

The Promise and Limits of Restorative Justice

In recent decades, an international movement for restorative justice (RJ) has held out the promise of a better way, one that stands in contrast to the retributive justice that nearly all nation-states impose. The movement offers an alternative vision of how a moral community might respond to victims of crime. In RJ the victim has fuller opportunity for her voice to be heard, the process is consensual rather than adversarial, and the remedy is restitution rather than "just deserts."

Australian criminologist John Braithwaite, a major theorist of this movement, describes the fundamental principle of restorative justice as repairing the harm of a crime rather than punishing offenders for breaking a law. "Because injustice hurts," he writes, "justice should heal." He defines the key values of RJ as nondomination, empowerment, and respectful listening. These are similar principles to those illustrated in the "Nonviolence Wheel" encountered in Chapter 2. Based on these fundamental principles, RJ processes can take many different forms. Braithwaite argues that rather than codifying specific processes, RJ should allow for many different variations in process to adapt to different cultural and institutional environments, both in criminal courts and beyond. These principles can also be implemented on vastly different scales, ranging from offenses against individual victims to mass atrocities, where RJ processes may serve as an alternative to war crimes tribunals in countries emerging from war and dictatorship. He argues that whereas punishment creates a vicious cycle of violence begetting violence, RJ offers at least the possibility of a virtuous cycle of "healing begetting healing."[4]

Although the practices of RJ have not been codified and are highly variable, two basic models are most common: conferencing and peace circles. Both are facilitated by an RJ practitioner and attended by, at minimum, the victim (called the harmed person), the perpetrator (called the harm-doer), and someone (possibly the facilitator) who represents the interests of the wider community. There is no standard number of people who may attend. Harm-doers and harmed persons may invite family and friends to attend as witnesses and supporters; the facilitator may also suggest others who are acceptable to both parties as community representatives. There are two primary preconditions: the harmed person has to give free, informed consent to participate in an RJ process, and the harm-doer has to acknowledge responsibility for what he has done. There is no fact-finding mechanism in RJ if the truth is disputed. The equivalent of a confession from the offender is required in order to allow the process to unfold.

In a peace circle, all participants sit together in a circle, and the facilitator passes around an object called the "talking piece." Only the person holding the talking piece may speak, while others listen without interrupting. The talking piece is passed around until everyone has had a chance to be heard. The process continues until the group reaches consensus about what should be done to repair the harm. In an RJ conference, the victim speaks first, telling her story and stating her wishes for amends. The offender is expected to offer his acknowledgment and apology and to state his willingness to make amends. The other witnesses also speak about how the crime has impacted them and what they would consider a fair resolution. Discussion continues until a workable restitution plan has been agreed upon. Clearly, one meeting alone cannot accomplish these ambitious goals, but there is no prescribed system either for working with participants before the face-to-face meeting or for implementation of the restitution plan. The facilitator guides the preparation for the meeting, and the follow-up plan is decided upon by consensus of the participants.

Braithwaite argues that the expression of righteous community indignation on behalf of the victim is an essential positive element of crime control. He criticizes both right- and left-wing positions on crime. He rejects both the punitive, "law-and-order" orientation traditionally associated with the prosecution and the permissive orientation traditionally associated with the defense bar. He is particularly critical of the traditional Left for its virtually exclusive focus on protecting the rights of the criminal defendant, a stance that offers no support to victims and no positive program for holding perpetrators accountable, effectively abandoning the crime issue to the Right.

Braithwaite proposes RJ as a third way; he advocates "vigorous moralizing about guilt, wrongdoing and responsibility, in which the harm-doer is confronted with community resentment and ultimately invited to come to terms with it."[5] Rather than ostracizing the offender and thereby hardening his antisocial attitudes, RJ offers a potential pathway back into community acceptance, through what Braithwaite calls reintegrative shaming. "Shaming," he writes, "is conceived . . . as a means of making citizens actively responsible, of informing them of how justifiably resentful their fellow citizens are toward criminal behavior which harms them. In practice, shaming surely limits autonomy, more surely than repression, but it does so by communicating moral claims."[6] This notion embraces an apparent contradiction; it envisions public rebuke and disgrace as a means not to humiliate and stigmatize harm-doers but rather to recognize their humanity and invite them to engage in repair.

In the conception of sophisticated theorists like Braithwaite, restorative justice principles offer the potential for vindication of the victim by the moral community that conventional justice so conspicuously lacks. Restorative practices such as conferences and healing circles also model the principles of mutuality, voice, and respect that are so rarely found in a courtroom. Restorative justice has been implemented most successfully, however, in circumstances where the moral community is in general agreement, both that the crime needs to be taken seriously and that repairing the harm might be a better solution than punishment.

Typical cases diverted to RJ involve single-incident, nonviolent property crimes such as theft or vandalism committed by young people. In these cases, where no one has been physically harmed, there is general consensus that harsh punishments are not in order and young people need a chance to make things right and learn from their mistakes.

When it comes to sexual assault or other forms of gender-based violence, however, the public is in fact divided. Supposedly, these are considered heinous crimes, deserving of severe punishment. But as we have seen in Chapter 3, these public attitudes apply only when the offender can be conveniently demonized according to popular prejudices and fantasies about who "counts" as a real criminal (a Black stranger, for example) and who "counts" as an "innocent" victim (a young blond woman who has never been on a date). In reality, since most offenders and victims do not fit these stereotypes, the public tends to blame the victim and recoil from punishing offenders. When crimes of violence are committed against subordinated or marginalized groups, punishment takes on important symbolic meaning in terms of how victims are valued in the wider community, as well as practical meaning in terms of how victims are protected from further harm. In these instances, restorative justice has been far more controversial.

At the grassroots level, the RJ movement has unfortunately reproduced many of the same deficiencies as the traditional justice system with respect to victims' rights. Many RJ programs have developed out of work with defendants in the criminal justice system, with the aim of finding alternatives to punishment. The concerns of victims have often been insufficiently represented, and the interests of victims may be subordinated to an ideological agenda just as easily as they are in the conventional system. In this instance, the agenda would be one of reconciliation and forgiveness rather than one of punishment.[7] Howard Zehr, a major theorist of the movement, admits that he initially viewed victims as a nuisance: "In my earlier work with prisoner defendants, I had not understood the perspectives of victims. Indeed, I did not want to, for they served primarily as interference in the process of finding 'justice' for the offender."[8]

Zehr's later work shows an evolution toward greater consideration for victims. He now asserts, "Victims must be key stakeholders rather than footnotes in the justice process."[9] This is an important advance. But unfortunately, the community called to bear witness to crimes of sexual violence in restorative justice practices is just as much a part of the patriarchal culture that sees victims as "footnotes" as any twelve jurors called upon to deliver a verdict within our conventional retributive system.

The restorative justice movement is a diverse coalition, building on adaptations of the practices of Indigenous peoples in North America, Australia, and New Zealand and bringing together progressive abhorrence of excessive punishment, radical pacifism, and a Christian doctrine of forgiveness. On the world stage, it was made famous by South Africa's Truth and Reconciliation Commission (TRC), led by Archbishop Desmond Tutu. As part of an agreement to end apartheid negotiated between the African National Congress and the Afrikaner government, amnesty was granted to the white perpetrators of violent political crimes in exchange for full confession. Many perpetrators (though not the top leadership) took advantage of this opportunity.

The perpetrators' confessions enabled the TRC to establish beyond dispute the ugly truth of apartheid's ruthless tyranny and made it impossible to create a successful revisionist narrative depicting white supremacy as benign. This in itself was a very important achievement. (For contrast, consider the sentimental portrayal of happy, loyal slaves and kind masters in *Gone with the Wind*, a masterpiece of "Lost Cause" propaganda and one of the most successful films of all time in the United States.) But the commission's greatest innovation was the centering of survivors' testimony. Many survivors told their stories in public hearings that were broadcast live on radio throughout the country. Archbishop Tutu's respectful and compassionate demeanor as he interviewed survivors modeled for the country the way to honor and vindicate survivors and to acknowledge the full truth and horror of the crimes committed against them.

The reconciliation agenda of the TRC was much less successful. Acknowledgment of the crimes of the apartheid regime was a necessary first step toward social repair and healing, but it soon became painfully clear that it was not a sufficient one. Absent was any form of public atonement or economic restitution. The majority-Black population remained in a state of dire poverty, just as, one hundred years earlier, the Black population in the United States was left destitute after the Civil War, denied the promised reparations (forty acres and a mule) for their centuries of forced labor.

As a young psychologist, Dr. Pumla Gobodo-Madikizele was a member of the Truth and Reconciliation Commission. She worked to seek out both victims and perpetrators and, when possible, to facilitate the kind of face-to-face encounters envisioned by restorative justice. She reported that many victims did want such an encounter but that most perpetrators (or their lawyers) refused, and she estimated that fewer than 5 percent of perpetrators were willing to apologize. She speculated that without the lawyers' intervention, that number might perhaps have been 20 percent, but still definitely a minority. In those rare cases when the perpetrators' remorse was genuine, some healing could occur, and those cases inspired hope. But in hindsight, years later, Dr. Gobodo-Madikizele (now a professor and well-known author) reflected that without reparations, general forgiveness was premature.[10]

In a paper titled "The Limits of Restorative Justice," Kathleen Daly, a professor of criminology in Australia, reviews a considerable body of evidence from courts in her country and in New Zealand, where RJ practices have been most widely implemented for juvenile offenders. She points out, first of all, that RJ is not a substitute for fact-finding; it can be implemented only when accused offenders voluntarily waive their right against self-incrimination and acknowledge their responsibility. Without a method of fact-finding (such as the presentation of conflicting evidence in an adversarial system), it can never entirely replace the conventional justice system. It is most useful in the penalty phase of the criminal process as a way to reenvision what the consequences of offending should be.

In the outcome studies that Daly reviews, most people who have participated in RJ, both offenders and victims, give the process high marks for fairness, but it is less common for offenders and victims to find common ground, and sincere apologies occur only in a minority of cases. She cites a study of an RJ project in New Zealand called RISE (Reintegrative Shaming Experiments), where the ideal of reconciliation and repair was reportedly achieved in less than half of all cases. Daly also points out that even in cases where the offender is sincerely remorseful, victims should not be expected or pressured to forgive. With these caveats, she concludes that "face-to-face encounters between victims and offenders *is* a practice worth maintaining, and perhaps enlarging, although we cannot expect it to deliver strong stories of repair and goodwill most of the time."[11] This seems like a balanced verdict: if justice is fairness, and both offenders and victims feel fairly treated in RJ processes, this is already an important accomplishment, even if the healing goals of RJ are not fully realized.

One Survivor's Experience

Kyra Jones, a Black artist, screenwriter, and community activist in Chicago, is a two-time survivor of sexual assault by men she knew. The first time this happened, when she was a college student at Northwestern University, she went to the police, but she found the criminal justice system totally alienating. The police were disrespectful, she reported, and no one ever once asked her what she wanted. This was an experience she knew she never wanted to repeat. So some years later, when she was raped once again by another man, she knew she had to find some other recourse.

Jones described Malcolm, the harm-doer, as a Black man and fellow community activist who "weaponized the language of the movement to target vulnerable women." She wanted him to acknowledge what had happened, and she wanted to warn her activist community about the ways he abused his positions of leadership, but she definitely did not want to report him to a criminal justice system that was all too ready to imprison Black men. She wanted him to acknowledge what he had done publicly in their shared peer group, but she understood that "when the threat of admitting what you did is being incarcerated, being enslaved, of course you're going to deny!" Like so many other survivors, she also wanted him to come to a full understanding of the harm he had done, to feel remorse, and to change his attitudes and his behavior so that he wouldn't harm anyone else.

For all these reasons, when Jones learned about an RJ alternative from Mariame Kaba, a revered Black writer-activist and experienced RJ practitioner in her community, she readily embraced it. Kaba, who presided over the planning and met regularly with Jones, assured her that Malcolm's acknowledgment and apology were requirements, but her forgiveness was not. Responding to social pressure from the activist community, Malcolm agreed to engage in the process, and a group of volunteers was engaged to prepare for a restorative justice peace circle. Support groups were organized both for Jones and for Malcolm. Jones's group helped her to process the trauma and develop her ideas for the kind of amends she wanted. Malcolm's group worked with him to help him understand the consequences of his actions and what kind of changes might be necessary to repair the harm he had done.

After fifteen months of regular meetings with his group, Malcolm was judged to be ready. He apologized for what he had done, agreed to everything that Jones asked for, and committed to a plan for "deep reflection and change." His support group committed to conducting regular follow-ups to be sure he was fulfilling his promises. Here was a perfect example of "reintegrative shaming" put into practice.

Unfortunately, after a year or two had elapsed, it became clear that Malcolm had continued to assault other women. At that point, some Black sexual assault survivors were angry with Jones for her choice *not* to file a criminal complaint. They thought Malcolm should have been in prison, where he would have been unable to hurt more women. Jones, a self-described "prison abolitionist," agonized over this: "What is the right answer?" she wondered aloud. Ultimately she decided that it was unfair to blame RJ for this failure. The responsibility belonged with Malcolm, she asserted, along with an activist community that had gone back to its default habits of valuing Black men over Black women.

There were a lot of activists who thought that the RJ process "fixed" him, and they started inviting him back into spaces where he could target and harm more Black women. They started giving him leadership roles again and allowing him to act like nothing ever happened, or in some cases put him on a pedestal because he went through the process. To put it more simply, it's like they knew he was a violent alcoholic, but decided it was fine to invite him to a bar because he went through AA.

In other words, the "moral community" constituted in the ad hoc fashion of restorative justice had not kept its part of the bargain. The shaming of the offender did not come from a deep enough culture of respect for women, and the reintegrative part had not entailed sufficient follow-up or care. In hindsight, Jones thought that at minimum Malcolm should have been permanently banned from leadership positions in any community organization.

Integrative Ideas

Kyra Jones's story illustrates many of the conundrums of restorative justice. The betrayal by bystanders can take many forms and can be especially painful in movements for social justice, where participants aspire to solidarity and "beloved community" but where patriarchal customs run deep. For this reason many feminists have expressed reservations about adapting RJ processes for crimes of violence against women. When community norms and beliefs are as divided and contentious as they are at present on matters of gender and power, it is hard to trust that community-based justice alternatives will be any more effective than the conventional justice system in addressing gender-based violence.

Beyond this conceptual problem, there are also problems of implementation. First is the problem of consistency. If we continue to believe that equal justice before the law is a principle worth upholding, it is hard to see how RJ practices can do so if each conference or peace circle comes up with its own idiosyncratic plan for accountability and restitution.

Then there is the problem of expense. Investing in "vigorous moralizing" with harm-doers turns out to be quite costly in terms of time and energy. It's not just a matter of a onetime meeting. Community participants are called upon as volunteers to devote many hours to the emotionally and intellectually demanding tasks of preparation and long-term follow-up. Anecdotal accounts of more successful cases indicate that weekly, intense meetings with a single offender and a single victim may go on for months or even years, with dropouts from exhaustion along the way.[12] Participation in an RJ process can be much more demanding than jury duty, which is probably the closest analog in our existing justice system. And many citizens find jury duty quite onerous, even with time off from work, and make all manner of excuses to get out of it.

Inexperience can also be a problem for volunteer RJ participants. Jurors may not be well versed in the law, but they have the judge to instruct them on the legal matters relevant to the case they are hearing. Having a wide range of citizens involved in the administration of justice for their peers is considered far more important than having expert jurors who understand the intricacies of the law. The same value of peer engagement inspires RJ volunteers, but in addition to playing the role of jurors, they are expected to be amateur social workers, psychologists, and probation officers. They need to come up with some sort of assessment of the harm-doer's dangerousness, the sincerity of his desire for change, and the likelihood of his rehabilitation.

They are expected to work with him to overcome his defensiveness and develop his capacity for empathy in preparation for the encounter with the person he has harmed. Finally, after the RJ encounter, they are expected to remain involved over the long term with the harm-doer, who may or may not remain cooperative, to assess whether he is truly "walking the walk" in his agreed-upon fulfillment plan or merely "talking the talk." Community shaming does not necessarily instill empathy for the victim or genuine remorse in the perpetrator, and community volunteers do not necessarily know how to supervise reintegration.

Finally, there is the issue of effective prevention of future harm. This is particularly important in the case of serial offenders and in cases such as trafficking and domestic violence, where a relationship of coercive control has been established between the offender and his victim. As we learned in Chapter 1, violence in such relationships is not an aberration but rather one of an integrated array of methods for maintaining dominance and part of a repetitive pattern. Advocates for battered women point out that abusers often woo their victims with profuse apologies after they have been violent, fostering the vain hope that the violence will cease and the relationship can be preserved. RJ, with its sentimental emphasis on apology and reconciliation, is thus tailor-made for manipulation by abusers. Well-meaning community volunteers cannot be expected to understand the power dynamics in abusive relationships or to recognize the many subtle ways in which abusers exert dominance over their victims. In such cases, RJ may actually serve to perpetuate abusers' power and control, exposing victims to additional danger.[13]

At present, the RJ movement is still too new to have amassed a convincing track record on preventing recidivism for violent crimes. This leaves survivors in a quandary as they consider taking a chance on RJ. As a group, the survivors whose testimonies are at the heart of this book were very ambivalent about punishment and even more so about incarceration. Among them, however, are six who went through with the complete criminal justice process to a final outcome of a conviction and a prison sentence for the offender. Several more would have been willing to do the same had prosecutors not declined to proceed. In these particular cases, the survivors felt that a prison term was necessary because they had seen up close how dangerous these men were, they wanted to protect other potential victims, and they didn't see any other way to do it.

As Sardina put it, "I did feel a sense of duty to go forward, because he was so bold, and he had no remorse. I felt sure he would do this again, and if he did, I couldn't live with myself. I realize in this case he may be a person who can't feel empathy, or he may have mental health issues. I would want to know if he's getting any treatment while incarcerated, and what he's doing to prevent this from happening again." She hoped that something would change him while he was in prison. In the meantime, however, she felt that prison was where he belonged.

Richard Wright, a Black activist and antiviolence organizer who witnessed domestic violence as a child, put it this way: "We have a saying in the community: some people should be locked up *under* the jail"—meaning that some offenders are too dangerous ever to be released; they need to be permanently removed from society.

On the other hand, advocates for RJ would argue that our current punitive system is both extremely expensive and actually quite ineffective. The expense of prosecutions, trials, and mass incarceration far exceeds what it might cost to provide adequate funding for a professional staff for well-designed RJ programs. And nothing in the prison system offers the prospect of true community safety. Incarceration simply incapacitates the offender for the duration of his sentence. Most incarcerated offenders are eventually released, with very high rates of re-offending. In fact, some critics argue that incarceration hardens first-time offenders and makes them *more* likely to reoffend once they are freed.

Many offenders might indeed be more receptive to intensive community-based efforts at rehabilitation than to confinement and ostracism. A small pilot study in the United States used Circles of Support and Accountability to assist imprisoned sex offenders at the expiration of their sentences. The researchers found that, compared to probation as usual, the restorative intervention both reduced reoffending and saved the state money.[14] A serious public investment in restorative justice might well allow more survivors to trust in this process and more offenders to reintegrate safely into their communities.

Legal scholars are increasingly recognizing the potential of RJ for crimes of violence. From the point of view of the defense bar, it offers an alternative to overly punitive sentencing and an incentive for offenders to admit what they have done. From the point of view of survivors, it offers greater voice and the promise of amends. From the point of view of the public, it offers at least a possibility of greater community safety, not to mention financial savings. Research on recidivism comparing RJ with the traditional criminal justice system is still in such an early stage that no firm conclusions can be drawn, but at the very least RJ seems to do no worse.[15] More and larger outcome studies are definitely needed.

A number of legal theorists now envision new ways to integrate RJ concepts and practices into the conventional justice system. Professor Ross London, whom we met in Chapter 2, proposes that the concept of just deserts for the offender can be made compatible with the basic principles of RJ, and he argues that some degree of retribution is necessary for serious crimes if RJ is to move out of its marginal niche and gain widespread public acceptance. "By adopting the view that the central contribution of restorative justice is its focus on repairing the harm of the crime," he writes, "we reject the view of restorative justice as a set of unique practices, thus enabling criminal justice planners to consider any number of practices that might achieve the goal of repair."[16] If some degree of punishment is accepted as a legitimate part of a restitution plan, he argues, restorative justice can potentially be adapted for a much wider range of offenses.

London envisions a court system in which a judge oversees the process, balancing the interests of the victim, the offender, and the community. From the bench of an imagined courtroom, this former judge addresses an imagined offender, saying, "Ask yourself a hard question: What can I possibly do to enable people to trust me again?" He envisions an RJ process in which the plan for making amends includes the offender's acceptance of some sanctions and hardships as a way of demonstrating his repentance, and he argues that rehabilitation is much more likely when the offender has some input into the restitution plan and agrees to the sanction rather than having it imposed by a judge.[17] In this manner, London envisions a justice system that is less harsh, less retributive, and fairer to all.

Australian criminologist Bronwyn Naylor also envisions a range of possible RJ approaches specifically for crimes of sexual violence. On one end of the spectrum is the purest and most radical form of RJ, sometimes called transformational justice, which takes place entirely outside the conventional justice system. This is the type of process in which Kyra Jones participated and which prison abolitionists like Mariame Kaba advocate.[18] At the other end of the spectrum would be a conventional court-based system in which RJ conferencing might be an option for making sentencing recommendations to the judge but is accessible only after an offender enters a formal guilty plea.

Naylor proposes a "middle way," a hybrid model "with formal court powers but more flexible and collaborative processes." She envisions a specialized sexual assault court, with well-trained judges and staff who understand the social dynamics of sexual violence. The RJ option would offer less punitive, more rehabilitative sanctions as incentives for offenders to participate, but would require a formal acknowledgment of responsibility and judicial oversight to ensure that the offender followed through with the redress plan. The plan itself would be worked out after adequate preparation in a conference organized and led by a professional facilitator. Having a judge sign off on the plan would hopefully ensure some degree of consistency and proportionality in sanctions. In conclusion, she argues that the conventional, adversarial justice system in place throughout the

English-speaking world has failed so profoundly to address sexual assault that it is time to consider what can be learned from more radical alternatives.[19]

Kyra Jones is still an advocate for RJ, and she remains a prison abolitionist. She invites us to imagine that just outcomes can be measured by the *survivor's* healing, whether or not the offender is healed. "Even though Malcolm re-offended," she writes, "I still came out of that process much healthier and armed with a community and resources that I would never have gotten without it."

This is exactly the point. Justice, from the perspective of my informants, was not centered on the question of the offender's fate; it was first and foremost about their *own* recovery. In their view, the primary obligation of the moral community was to help repair the harm that had been done to *them* and only then to figure out what to do about the offenders. Survivors' visions of justice combine retributive and restorative elements in the service of healing a damaged relationship, not primarily between victims and offenders but rather between victims and the bystanders in their communities. In other words, survivors' justice demands that when a person has been harmed, the first duty of the moral community is to support and care for her. When the community embraces the survivor, justice is served.

The question then becomes what to do about the offender. This is a problem for the whole community to struggle with. Survivors alone cannot solve it; nor should that be their responsibility, though they have certainly given it a great deal more serious thought than most bystanders. My informants were virtually unanimous in their wish to see the offenders publicly exposed and disgraced. This could be considered retributive, of course, but as my informants elaborated their motives in the interviews, it became clear that the main purpose of exposure was not to "get even" by inflicting pain. Rather, they hoped that exposure of the offenders would mobilize the community to recognize the truth, to rebuke the offenders, and to figure out whatever steps were necessary to prevent the offenders from harming others in the future.

The restorative element of the survivors' vision was most apparent in their focus on the harm of the crime rather than on the abstract violation of the law and in their preference for making things as right as possible in the future rather than avenging the past. Their vision was restorative, also, in their emphasis on the importance of community acknowledgment and denunciation of the crime. Their focus, however, was primarily on their own need for healing, safety, and reintegration with their communities rather than on the offenders' need for reintegration. They recognized that the community had to find a way to reach offenders, but first they needed the community to embrace them and relieve them of their own burdens of silencing and shame.

Accountability for Complicit Institutions

In addition to their desire to hold individual offenders accountable, survivors fervently wished to hold accountable the institutions that had actively enabled, protected, and covered up for the offenders. "Daniel," a survivor of childhood sexual abuse by one of the most notorious of the pedophile priests in the Archdiocese of Boston, was working as a counselor for troubled adolescents and participating in a civil suit against the archdiocese when I interviewed him in 2002. As more and more survivors came forward around the country and then around the world, the church faced numerous civil suits for damages. In this instance, survivors in many dioceses qualified to file class-action lawsuits in the United States. Daniel's suit ultimately resulted in a landmark settlement: in 2004 the Archdiocese of Boston agreed to pay damages of $85.4 million for claims representing 552 victims against 140 priests.[20] At present it is estimated that the church has paid somewhere in the neighborhood of several billion dollars to settle civil claims, with no end in sight.

Daniel spoke about the different forms of accountability that he imagined for the perpetrator and for the church hierarchy. When we discussed his desired consequences for the perpetrator, Father Paul Shanley, Daniel began by quoting his best friend, who offered to "cut off the priest's ears and return them." Daniel thought that was "a sweet thing to say, but that's not what I'm interested in." He added, "I don't even believe in the prison aspect of our criminal justice system." Daniel was more interested in getting treatment for the perpetrator than seeing him punished. "What's most important is that he doesn't do it again," Daniel said. "Probably that means jail, since there's no place for people like him. I know that sex offenders are difficult to treat. Some of the kids I work with are sex offenders. He would need an indefinite sentence until he is judged not dangerous. And not by a parole board that said he did his laundry, but by a psychologist who says he's a minimal danger." (Father Paul Shanley was in fact convicted of child rape in 2004 and sentenced to twenty years in prison. He appealed his conviction, which the Supreme Court of Massachusetts upheld. He served twelve years, was released with ten years' probation, and died of a heart attack in 2020.)

Daniel then explained why he was so angry with the Catholic Church. It had come to light that the Archdiocese of Boston had known about Father Paul's pedophile habits since at least 1993, when he was sent for an inpatient psychiatric evaluation and admitted to having had sex with multiple young boys in his parish in the 1980s. The church had then quietly settled several lawsuits, with nondisclosure agreements, and transferred Father Paul to a parish in California. "He's sick and he's dangerous," Daniel said, "and they knew that, and they didn't do anything about it. They kept assigning him to places where he would be with kids, and they kept not notifying people, and they kept having people who sued them sign confidentiality agreements, and the list goes on and on . . . I want to go punch them in the face, and I'm not a violent person. *They should have known better.*"

Asked how the church should be held accountable, Daniel said vehemently, "They could start by apologizing for the Crusades and move forward from there." By this I believe he meant that a religious institution capable of sending its faithful into "holy wars" of conquest was capable of every other kind of atrocity as well. He understood that the autocratic nature of the church hierarchy led inevitably to abuses of power, and therefore he wanted to see its most powerful representatives brought low. Speaking of Cardinal Bernard Law, who had for years knowingly covered up the systemic child abuse in the Archdiocese of Boston, Daniel said, "I'd like to see him stripped of his position of authority, his big diamond ring and his scepter and all that. I'd like to see him really do work, something humbling. A thousand years of community service that's not schmoozing, not fun, not glamorous. I kind of want to see him in jail, just for a few weeks, just to feel the consequences. They should sell his mansion and give the proceeds to victims."

Daniel's vision of accountability was echoed in "A Call to Reform the Archdiocese of Boston," the 2003 consensus document put together by a group of survivors. In addition to their demand for a public confession of responsibility, they asked for many "observable actions" to show that the church was serious about making fair and just amends to survivors. They asked for ethical settlement of civil lawsuits, with an immediate end to "hardball tactics" and nondisclosure agreements. They asked that the church cease lobbying in state legislatures against extending the statute of limitations for criminal cases so that survivors would have more opportunity to come forward and more priests could be held accountable in court. They also asked that the church endow a full-service mental health center for survivors that would be run entirely independently of the archdiocese, supervised by a board of directors composed of trauma experts and survivors. They asked that the church endow secure retirement homes where sex offenders would be confined and allowed to leave only with supervision. And they asked that all members of the clergy commit to engage in regular reflection and training about the dynamics of power and its abuses.

When the document was completed, the group sent a letter requesting a meeting to present it to Archbishop Seán Patrick O'Malley, Cardinal Law's successor, who had often publicly stated that he would meet with survivors anywhere and at any time. This and two subsequent requests were refused. The group then wrote a statement titled "Three Times Denied," denouncing the archbishop for turning his back on those who had suffered.[21] Thus the tragedy of betrayal was reenacted by the institution built on the rock of St. Peter.

Peter repented bitterly of his cowardice in denying Jesus and prayed for forgiveness. Penitence from the church has been much less apparent. Though, over two decades, the church has settled hundreds of civil claims for damages, and these monetary reparations have certainly benefited survivors, it has yet to reckon in any serious way with its institutional responsibility at the highest levels for sheltering and covering up what amounted to a clandestine international pedophile ring. The pope did appoint a task force to study the problem and even invited survivor representatives to participate, but before long they resigned, saying they did not wish to be used as window dressing for an effort that they did not believe would lead to any meaningful change. Cardinal Law did find it convenient to get out of Boston for the friendlier environs of the Vatican after the *Boston Globe*'s Spotlight investigation revealed the depths of his complicity with these crimes, but he was never held accountable in any of the ways Daniel and many other survivors would have wished. He may not have kept his scepter and his big diamond ring, and he never did fulfill his rumored lifelong ambition of becoming the first American pope, but he lived out his days in luxury and comfort in Rome, as the archpriest at the venerable Basilica of Santa Maria Maggiore, attended by nuns. When it comes to accountability for institutional enablers of criminal violence, we are a long way from survivors' justice.

Few institutions can rival the Roman Catholic Church in its extraordinary wealth, its organizational complexity, and its estimated 1.3 billion adherents worldwide. But one that may come close is the sex trade. Comparing the two institutions may seem strange, even outrageous; one promises the eternal bliss of salvation in the hereafter while the other promises more immediate earthly pleasures. But both share a rigid patriarchal ideology and an opaque authoritarian structure that fosters secrecy and enables criminal exploitation. Just as civil law has recently been used to begin holding the Catholic Church accountable for its institutional complicity in child sexual abuse, a creative use of civil law could also potentially begin holding some components of the global sex industry accountable for their numerous abuses of power.

In one notable lawsuit, filed in federal court in June 2021, plaintiffs Serena Fleites, a victim of sex trafficking, and Jane Doe Nos. 1 through 33, citizens of the United States, Canada, the United Kingdom, Colombia, and Thailand, charge the corporation MindGeek, owner of Pornhub, as well as several subsidiary porn purveyors, with harms due to violations of both civil and criminal law. Pornhub is the world's biggest marketer of online pornography. The suit also names as defendants Feras Antoon, the CEO of MindGeek, and Bernd Bergmair, its principal financier. These gentlemen apparently have gone to some lengths to keep their names and activities unknown to the public. The complaint includes sex trafficking; receipt, transport, and distribution of child pornography; and racketeering. All of these are federal crimes. The great advantage of using civil rather than criminal law, however, is the fact that survivors can initiate the complaint rather than waiting for federal prosecutors, who may or may not be interested in such an undertaking, to do so. In addition, the complaint includes several violations of civil laws, such as distribution of private sexually explicit materials.

The suit is also notable in that it names the credit card company Visa as a codefendant, arguing that by enabling credit card payment online, the company knowingly enables criminal conduct. Negative publicity has already compelled Visa and MasterCard to stop processing direct payments for downloading videos from Pornhub. This represents a considerable financial blow to Pornhub, even though the credit card companies have quietly found workarounds, by allowing payment for advertising on Pornhub's website.

The lead attorney on the case, Michael J. Bowe of Brown, Rudnick, LLP, has in the past successfully pursued settlements in cases of money laundering and organized crime. This is the kind of lawsuit in which attorneys from prominent law firms represent their clients on a pro bono or contingency basis, knowing that their clients have no money but that the defendants have enormous fortunes. Should their suit prevail, the law firm stands to gain a substantial portion of what could be many millions of dollars in damages awarded by the court. Major law firms also have the financial resources to conduct the kind of in-depth investigative work that may often be necessary to pursue cases of this kind, and in this regard they may actually be better resourced than many federal prosecutors.

In its introductory statement, the complaint reads as follows: "MindGeek is the most dominant online pornography company in the world. It is also one of the largest human trafficking ventures in the world. . . . The defendants succeeded in creating a bustling marketplace for child pornography, rape videos, trafficked videos, and every other form of non-consensual content. . . . That business plan worked. And the MindGeek defendants got rich."[22]

Since this is a civil lawsuit, the consequences for the defendants, should the suit prevail, are measured only in dollars for reparations to the victims, not in criminal punishments. However, if the suit reaches the phase of discovery, relevant documents can be subpoenaed and must be handed over to the court. Defendants must also submit to depositions; that is, they must respond under oath to questions posed by the plaintiffs' counsel. Thus, the case has the potential to expose many of the clandestine workings of this international enterprise, and this in turn could lead to serious criminal liabilities for the defendants.

My colleague Melissa Farley, a psychologist who is the executive director and founder of Prostitution Research and Education and who brought this lawsuit to my attention, estimates that MindGeek and the other defendants will obtain the services of the toughest, most expensive lawyers they can find and that they will play "hardball" for as long as they can, just as the various dioceses of the Catholic Church have done. The first maneuver is always to try to get the case thrown out in a summary judgment. If that strategy fails, however, it is in the defendants' interest to settle out of court for a large sum of money rather than expose the inner workings of their organizations to daylight.[23] As of this writing, in June 2022, Serena Fleites's attorneys have refiled her case separately at the instruction of the judge, and they have already filed for discovery. In addition,

MindGeek is now also facing four active class-action lawsuits (two in the United States and two in Canada) on behalf of survivors whose images were used without their consent. Also in June 2022, soon after an article about the lawsuits against Pornhub appeared in the *New Yorker* magazine, Antoon, the CEO, and David Tassillo, the chief operating officer of Mind-Geek, announced their retirement. MindGeek denies that this change of leadership has anything to do with the company's legal difficulties.

One of the US cases has already advanced to the discovery phase, which means that a settlement offer is likely. The plaintiffs and their attorneys will then have to decide whether to accept a monetary settlement or to try to hold out for the kinds of institutional changes that are so much harder to get.

The offer of money damages almost always creates inner conflict for survivor plaintiffs. On the one hand, survivors may need the money desperately. Moreover, the award of damages does represent some kind of acknowledgment and vindication, as well as reparation, the most basic forms of justice. On the other hand, many survivors feel tainted by financial compensation, as though they had been "bought." For women whose bodies have indeed been paid for, this conflict is particularly intense.

Also, as we saw in the case of Ross Cheit in Chapter 4, survivors want many other kinds of accountability and amends besides money from institutions that enabled and covered up criminal practices. A few particularly notorious offenders may be held accountable once in a while, but any damages awarded can often simply be factored into the institution's cost of doing business, which then continues as usual. True accountability requires the profound institutional changes that would prevent the repetition of these crimes in the future.

We turn now to an exploration of how amends to survivors might be expanded and implemented in a way that actively removes the taint of receiving "dirty money," repairs the relationship between survivors and their communities, and fosters institutional change.

PART THREE

HEALING

7

RESTITUTION

What, you think all I want is money? What, you think *money* can ever repay what you stole?

—Ashley M. Jones, "Reparations Now! Reparations
Tomorrow! Reparations Forever!"[1]

How can perpetrators and communities make amends to survivors for their suffering? Traditionally, in the justice system, survivors can seek reparations from perpetrators in the form of monetary damages in civil court. But as we learned in Chapter 4, survivors face many practical obstacles if they attempt to gain this form of justice. In effect, it takes money to get money, since legal representation is expensive except in the event that the perpetrator is so wealthy that a lawyer will take the case on contingency. It also takes a lot of courage to engage in an adversarial contest that may drag out for months or years. Also, as we learned in the case of Ross Cheit (Chapter 4), even a court ruling in favor of the plaintiff may be only a symbolic victory if the defendant doesn't have any money.

Beyond all these practical difficulties, however, is a larger, conceptual issue: money is not the main thing that most survivors think of when they try to imagine what would make things right for them. It may come as a surprise, for instance, that only a minority of the survivors whom I interviewed expressed any wish for direct monetary damages from the men who had harmed them. Some said that no amount of money could compensate for the harm; for them, the idea of monetary damages felt almost like a vulgar insult. Others said that accepting money from the perpetrator would make them feel compromised, as though they had been bought off. The artist Amy Bradford, whom we met in Chapter 5, sued the man who raped her in civil court after criminal prosecution was denied. For her, monetary damages were symbolic. She asked that he be required to contribute $30 to the local rape crisis center. In her mind, the money represented the thirty pieces of silver for which Judas betrayed Jesus. Much to my astonishment, she didn't care about the fact that he was wealthy and could have afforded a much larger payment. (The rapist paid the $30.)

Many survivors did speak bitterly of the financial losses they had incurred as a result of their traumas, not only in the cost of medical and mental health care but also in lost years and derailed careers, and some felt that an award of financial restitution would have been only right. Lybia Rivera, whom we met in Chapter 4, reflected on what justice would mean for her. She wanted some sort of rehabilitation both for the neighbor who sexually abused her when she was a child and for the professor who sexually harassed her when she was a graduate student. But she also wanted her abusers to have to pay to repair the harm they had done. "Trauma is a life sentence," she said. "When you get raped it affects your whole life, from that moment on. How much money have I spent on doctors and hospitals! Years of treatment! I think that's very unfair. I wish there would be an institution that would be an arbiter, so that the person who committed the rape would have to pay for life. The money would be taken out of his paycheck, like taxes."

Something like what Rivera envisioned does exist in the United States, although this fact isn't widely known outside the community of victim services. The 1984 Victims of Crime Act (VOCA) offers a progressive model of reparations, both to individual victims and to the community. The law was passed during the presidency of Ronald Reagan, who promoted it as part of a "law and order," anti-crime agenda. VOCA establishes a national trust fund to serve victims, supported not by general taxpayer funds but rather by fines assessed on convicted offenders. Victim representatives are invited to serve on the federal and state boards that determine priorities for allocating the money. The funds have been used over the years, first, to compensate individual victims for time lost from work and medical bills incurred as a result of a crime; second, to pay for victim advocacy services in criminal courts; and finally, to support grassroots community service agencies like rape crisis centers and battered women's shelters.

In this manner, perpetrators *as a group* are required by the community to make amends to victims *as a group*, without a need for face-to-face encounters between individual perpetrators and victims. In this sense, I would call it progressive. Financial restitution may feel more acceptable to victims, less like "dirty money," when it comes from a general trust fund mandated and implemented by the community rather than from the particular person who harmed them. Having a pooled trust fund also allows for a victim to be appropriately compensated regardless of whether the particular person who harmed her is rich or poor. The legislation also empowers victims by granting them a voice in deciding, along with other members of the community, what is most needed for restitution.

In a report evaluating the effectiveness of the VOCA approach, a nonprofit organization called the National Center for Victims of Crime found that the program was very helpful as far as it went but was underutilized and underfunded. They proposed that it be expanded by including taxpayer contributions as well as fines on offenders as sources of funding. They argued that the state, as the guarantor of public safety, shared the responsibility for restitution. "One important way to fulfill this obligation," they wrote, "is through financial assistance that represents a public acknowledgment of the wrong done to victims of crime, recognizes the harm experienced by victims, and helps alleviate the financial consequences of the crime."[2] Note that the report echoes the sentiments of my informants, naming acknowledgment, vindication, and repair as the most important elements of healing the relationship between the victim and the community.

This brings us to the larger issue of what restitution means to survivors above and beyond monetary damages imposed on perpetrators. Many survivors understand that their suffering is not simply a personal misfortune but rather the result of a larger social problem. Because they know that many people in their communities enabled the abuse that they endured, they seek community amends in the form of institutional and cultural change. Here we will review a number of instances in which particular cases led to wider institutional changes.

Healing Justice in the Workplace

In cases of sexual harassment, restitution can take the form of creating a workplace environment of safety, and this in turn may require removing offenders from positions of power. At present, it seems that multiple complaints are required before any kind of institutional response can be expected, and civil litigation, or at least the threat of it, may be necessary. This has been the experience of the many women who came forward in the #MeToo movement to expose some of the most egregious workplace behavior of powerful men. It was also the experience of "Rose," whom we first met as a young rape survivor in Chapter 4. A decade after this trauma, when she began a new teaching job at a state college, Rose was targeted by a senior member of the faculty. "Do you know how hard it is to get a white male tenured professor fired?" she asked.

As Rose tells the story, the professor's harassment began with his commenting to all and sundry, "The new hire is so hot!" No one said a word; apparently he was well known for this kind of behavior. But Rose was no longer as defenseless as she had been as a teenager. "I became furious," she said, "and I wrote down every single interaction over eighteen months." When she had collected her evidence, she consulted a lawyer, who told her she had enough documentation for a civil suit. Then she went to her department chairperson, the union, and eventually the dean of the college. After Rose started speaking up, five other women came forward. "I had all the tools I needed," she said. "I went to the dean and named conditions at 3:00 on a Tuesday afternoon. The next morning at 8:00 a.m. the dean said he found the money for mandatory trainings on sexual harassment and bystander intervention, and this guy got removed in the middle of the semester."

Rose's success in this case depended first of all on her courage in speaking up and the courage of the other women who came forward. Their collective action in turn was made possible by all the "tools" that Rose had at her disposal, tools developed over four decades of feminist pioneering in sexual harassment law. There was more to the tale, of course. The professor appealed his suspension through the institutional hierarchy, claiming it was "reverse discrimination" and that his treatment of Rose couldn't possibly be sexual harassment because, after all, she was his daughter's age. Nevertheless, her complaint was upheld on each appeal. "Even the chancellor believed me!" Rose reported. She observed that the required faculty trainings have resulted in better behavior and a better workplace atmosphere for the next generation. "It's been cool. It opened up conversations about sexual harassment, and it has empowered me since they ruled in my favor," she reflected. "In this way, justice can be really validating."

Note that Rose's demands for repair did not include any money damages for herself; rather, she sought disciplinary action from her institution to prevent the perpetrator from continuing in his position of power and financial investment in faculty education to change the culture that tolerated or condoned abuses of power. This could be considered a successful example of survivors' justice.

Note also that the "tools" that Rose had at her disposal are still relatively weak compared to the weight of patriarchal tradition and institutional inertia. Creating a strong enough evidence record to prevail still took the complaints of six women, legal counsel, and eighteen months' worth of documentation.

In my own university, a recent sexual harassment case illustrated just how much power a tenured white male professor can still bring to bear. In this instance, when Harvard, after investigating multiple complaints, put a prominent professor on unpaid administrative leave, over thirty of his very prominent faculty colleagues signed a support letter for him *without knowing the facts of the case.* The dean of the faculty, to her credit, called them out for this, and most of them sheepishly withdrew their signatures a few days later. Shortly afterward, three women who had been his students filed a civil complaint against Harvard in federal court, claiming that the university had ignored the professor's notorious behavior for years and citing the professor's ability to mobilize his colleagues' unquestioning support as evidence of his power to blacklist them professionally.[3] Apparently, Harvard is also much in need of the kind of faculty education that Rose was able to gain as restitution for herself and so many other survivors.

Healing Justice: Grassroots Initiatives

Creating effective healing services for survivors often requires integrating systems that tend to operate in separate silos. Police, prosecutors, courts, and social services generally have very different cultures. Yet clearly, without well-established cooperation, none of these components is capable of responding by itself to the complexities of gender-based violence. Sometimes grassroots survivor advocacy organizations, which of necessity interface with all these institutions, can take the lead to bridge these divides.

An illustration comes from my home city of Cambridge, Massachusetts, which recently published its "Guide for a Trauma-Informed Law Enforcement Initiative," developed through a collaboration between the city's police department and its Domestic and Gender-Based Violence Prevention Initiative. This manual is based on a model that has been in place in Cambridge for several years. It describes a three-day training for police officers, to be repeated at regular intervals. The aims of the training are threefold: first, to help the officers understand their own exposures to trauma and promote their own mental health; second, to help officers understand the impact of trauma on the victims of violence whom they frequently encounter in crisis situations like domestic violence so that they will respond with less prejudice and more compassion; and finally, to improve relations between the police and the general public by teaching officers how to treat survivors of violence with more respect and understanding throughout the process of criminal investigation.

In implementing similar trainings in other communities, the authors of this guide recommend that a city or town planning committee should include community representatives and trauma specialists along with police department leadership. They note that most police departments have "some tension between a traditional 'law and order' or military culture and a more social service orientation." They warn the teams delivering the training to "anticipate and respect potential resistance to what may be seen as 'soft' content," and they strongly suggest that the police department leadership commit to attending the entire training in order to demonstrate support from the top of the hierarchy. If the bosses don't attend, the rank and file will most likely conclude that the trainings are not really important and approach them with a cynical attitude.[4]

Psychologist Barbara Hamm, a colleague from the Victims of Violence Program who participated in some of the early police trainings in Cambridge, told me that she did indeed encounter resistance to "soft" concepts, particularly the idea that the first responders who frequently encounter violence might be suffering themselves and might need to attend to their own self-care. Younger officers seemed receptive but expressed concern that any acknowledgment of their posttraumatic symptoms might make them appear weak, and they were afraid that any show of vulnerability might subject them to ridicule from some of their peers and to harsh criticism from their supervisors, whom they called the "old bulls." Clearly the traditional police culture, which demanded constant performance of stereotypic masculine toughness, was harmful to the officers themselves as well as to the people in the community whom they were called upon to serve.[5]

This example from the Cambridge Police Department illustrates how the concept of healing justice expands from the center of what survivors need for repair to recognition of the need for healing throughout the entire social ecology of violence, including the culture of the first responders. An evaluation of the training program showed that participants increased their ability to identify signs of trauma and their confidence that they could use their newly learned interviewing and investigation methods to protect victims from further traumatization. Crucially, they also felt more confident that their agency would support them when they changed the way they treated crime victims, based on their greater understanding of trauma. These encouraging initial data bolster the hope that changing the culture of policing will ultimately benefit survivors as well and will represent a form of community repair.

For another example of the myriad ways that healing justice can expand the ecological frame, consider the story of an organization called Have Justice—Will Travel (HJWT), a legal multiservice center founded by a remarkable attorney named Wynona Ward. Raised in poverty in a large family on a dirt road in rural Vermont, Ward described her father as a "patriarch" who was extremely violent to her mother and both physically and sexually abused all five children in the family. She married young and partnered with her husband as a long-distance truck driver. During her husband's driving shifts, she studied for her college degree in the back of the truck. After graduation, she won a scholarship to Vermont Law School.

Ward's survivor mission was to use her knowledge of the law to help battered women like her mother and survivors of sexual abuse like herself and her siblings. She understood that the power of the law alone would be necessary but not sufficient. To illustrate this, when I first interviewed her twenty years ago, soon after she founded HJWT, she told the story of one of her first clients, a woman much like her mother, living on a back road with no telephone and no driver's license. Ward drove out to meet with the client, offering her legal services in her home. The first step was to help the client get a permanent restraining order and then a court order granting her custody of the children, with supervised visitation and child support. But those legal protections were just the beginning. Ward recognized that establishing real safety required much more than court orders. This client also needed help gaining housing in town, in a place where she would not be isolated. She needed help enrolling in a program to get her GED. She needed to learn how to drive. And most of all, she needed to get her teeth fixed. Her abuser had knocked out her front teeth, and she felt terribly ashamed of her appearance. Ward understood the symbolic importance of the missing teeth, which stigmatized her client as stereotypical "trailer trash," and she helped her client find a dentist who would accept Medicaid payments.

A year after that first home visit, Ward reported that her client had a job working as the manager of a small retail store. Walking into that store, she said she almost didn't recognize her client. "She had a different stance. Proud, like 'I'm somebody. I've gotten somewhere.'" True justice, to Ward, meant not only gaining legal protection for victims of violence but also enabling them to recover and thrive. It meant bringing the powers of the law from the courthouse to the people. One might think of this as a practice of community law.

Twenty years after its founding, Have Justice—Will Travel has grown and prospered in Vermont. Ward is still the director. The organization's mission is still to work with rural victims of domestic and sexual violence, providing legal services, transportation, and in-home or safe-area consultation, so that victims can achieve independence. When I interviewed Ward again recently, she reviewed the changes of the last twenty years. She reported that half the judges in Vermont are now women and that has made a difference. "They're well trained now, and they recognize that when people have been through trauma, they need to listen and understand." But she also acknowledged that a translation gap still remains between her clients' lived experience and the language of the law. That's why legal representation is still so necessary and why poor women still need attorneys.

Imagine if services like HJWT were the standard in every community. This would represent a true commitment to survivors' safety and healing and a true form of restitution to survivors.

Healing Justice: Changing the Courts

Initiatives to change the social ecology of response to survivors can sometimes come from within the courts themselves. In one remarkable example, a criminal court judge, the Honorable Fernando Camacho, organized a special diversion court called the Human Trafficking Intervention Court for young people arrested for prostitution in Queens County, New York, a model program that has now been replicated in many other jurisdictions. In this instance, change began with the judge's gradual recognition that these girls were indeed victims, not criminals.

In an article titled "Sexually Exploited Youth: A View from the Bench," Judge Camacho writes about the misconceptions that pervade the criminal justice system regarding prostitution, misconceptions that he shared for many years, starting out in 1985 as an assistant district attorney in Manhattan. Most of his colleagues, in law enforcement, in the district attorney's office, and on the bench, assumed that women in "the Life" were consenting adults, "bad girls" who made "bad choices" of their own free will. The reality, he explains, is quite different. "Over the last several years," he writes, "I have vacated numerous criminal convictions of girls who were eleven, twelve, and thirteen years old when they took adult pleas. They lied about their ages on the instruction of their pimps. . . . The ugly truth is that many of those charged with prostitution are in fact kids."[6]

Judge Camacho then explains how pimps recruit the most vulnerable young people, abused kids who are runaways or throwaways, mostly Black and brown girls, and how the pimps' methods of coercive control make it extremely difficult for their victims to escape once they are entrapped. He describes one memorable scene from his courtroom when a young woman, who had had the temerity to complain to the police after her pimp gave her a beating, was sitting in the first row waiting to testify. The pimp entered the courtroom, walked up to the young woman, and knocked her out cold in the presence of court officers, attorneys, and "one bewildered judge." With this bold action, the pimp sent a message to his victim and to all the bystanders: "*I own you and no one can protect you from me*—not the police, not the prosecutor, and certainly not the person in the black robe."[7]

Finally, one day in 2003, Judge Camacho had had enough. When a sixteen-year-old runaway named Siobhan appeared before him on what was at least her fifth arrest for prostitution, with the dead eyes he had come to recognize in so many kids, he decided not to sentence her to the usual twenty days in jail. Instead, he referred her to Girls Educational & Mentoring Services (GEMS), a grassroots social service and self-help organization for girls in the Life. Soon he organized a regular collaboration with GEMS and its founder, Rachel Lloyd, herself a survivor, and he also began a partnership with the rape crisis center at St. Vincent's Hospital. He never again sentenced anyone to jail for prostitution, though he continued to encourage the prosecution of pimps, whom he regarded as the real criminals in the business of prostitution.

The beginning was difficult. Judge Camacho still remembers "snickers and whispers" from his colleagues when he first began his program. With no funding, he simply asked other judges to send their prostitution cases to his court. He "borrowed" a case manager from the neighboring drug court and arranged with graduate programs in law and social work to send him student interns. "We had to break down barriers, educate people," he said. "It's such a difficult topic to get your head around. It's so painful to listen to the suffering; people would rather ignore it."[8] He persisted, however, and slowly he expanded collaboration between victim advocates and prosecutors. "The curtain of shamefulness started to lift, and law enforcement and prosecutors began to see trafficked individuals for who they actually are—victims and not criminals."[9] By diverting trafficked people to services instead of jail, he spared them punishment and offered them instead a chance to escape from prostitution.

The success of the Human Trafficking Intervention Court gradually convinced many skeptics, and eventually this diversion court became a model for implementation statewide and beyond. A documentary film titled *Blowin' Up* shows a bustling courtroom, filled with young women sitting on the benches awaiting their turn or conferring with their court-appointed lawyers in the hallways.[10] The court provides translators who speak Spanish, Chinese, Korean, and many other languages. The Honorable Toko Serita, who succeeded Judge Camacho, presides with a calm, businesslike, but kindly demeanor. She estimates that at its height, the court saw from five hundred to six hundred cases per year.

I asked Judge Camacho what he considered the essential requirements for replicating the success of his court. He replied that there was no formula; it was all about talking with people. In his view, there was no substitute for the hard work of building personal relationships with people who approached the concrete practices of the justice system from many different perspectives: the judges, the district attorneys, the public defenders, the police, and the victim advocates. We hear this theme repeatedly from those who seek to make changes in the justice system: building a new moral community that does not as yet exist requires community organizing, bringing together people who ordinarily do not talk to one another, and building trust based on a shared commitment to seeking a better way.

Like Wynona Ward at Have Justice—Will Travel, both Judge Camacho and Judge Serita report that they have seen changes in public attitudes and court practices over the last two decades since the founding of the Human Trafficking Intervention Court. High-profile cases and press attention helped to change long-held prejudices. *New York Times* columnist Nick Kristof began writing about the degradation inherent in sex trafficking. The governor of New York was arrested in a prostitution scandal. Similar celebrity cases also gained press attention. In Boston, when New England Patriots owner Robert Kraft was arrested and charged with buying sex, the *Boston Globe* published "Dear 'Johns'—an Open Letter to Sex Buyers," written by three teenage trafficking survivors, identified only by their initials. "The real story here," they wrote, "is not one man. The real story is all of you who think it is acceptable to buy someone." They wanted the johns to know that they were human beings, not toys or sex objects, and that being in the Life was dehumanizing. "Now you know," they concluded. "You can no longer pretend that you don't. . . . It is demand that fuels this multibillion-dollar industry. If you didn't buy people, people wouldn't sell people."[11] Judge Serita estimates that "public awareness is evolving the way awareness of domestic violence was 20 years ago."[12]

As this profoundly different view of sex trafficking has gradually gained credence, legal reforms have begun to follow. Judge Camacho cites particularly New York's 2007 anti-trafficking act, which focused on the crimes of the traffickers, and the 2008 Safe Harbor for Exploited Children Act, which created a presumption that minors arrested for prostitution were trafficking victims. He cautions, however, that the very success of the diversion courts may have contributed to an organized and apparently well-funded backlash seeking to decriminalize the prostitution industry entirely—meaning that the pimps and johns, as well as the people whose bodies are sold, would no longer be subject to arrest or criminal charges.

This brings us to a major controversy in contemporary feminist thought: What is to be done about prostitution? On one side we find those who might be called neoliberal or libertarian or "sex-positive" feminists, who advocate complete decriminalization of the sex industry, allowing market forces to rule.[13] Liberals want to put an end to oppressive policing and remove the stigma and degradation attached to the sex trade by normalizing it as just another kind of work. This would be considered a "harm-reduction" approach, the hope being that, freed from the threat of criminal prosecution, "sex workers" would also be free from pimps and brothel keepers, who offer them "protection," and could keep the money they earn from their own independent small businesses.

On the other side are the radical feminists, who aspire to abolish the sex trade entirely, arguing that it is inherently exploitative, preying on the most vulnerable women and children. They maintain that "happy hookers" are a fiction of sex-trade propaganda. Let's face it: no little girl aspires to have strangers, or even regular clients, ejaculate into her bodily orifices ten to twelve times per night when she grows up (or, more realistically, when she turns eleven, twelve, or thirteen). For this reason, these latter-day abolitionists argue that selling other people's bodies is indeed and should continue to be a serious crime.

A radical alternative to legalized prostitution originated in the Swedish sex-purchase laws of 1999. Under these laws, the sex buyer, the trafficker, and other third parties who profit from the transaction (i.e., the john, the pimp, and the brothel keeper) are subject to criminal penalties, but the prostituted person is not. These laws are based not on prudish claims of protecting public morals but rather on an analysis of social hierarchy that recognizes the extreme asymmetry in power between prostituted people and those who buy or market their services. The so-called Nordic model, pioneered in Sweden, has now been adopted in several other countries, including Iceland, Norway, Canada, France, Northern Ireland, the Republic of Ireland, and Israel. In practice, though the law allows for sentences of up to one year in prison, the penalties for most johns are fines. The Swedish law also provides for public education about the harms of prostitution and extensive reparative services for prostituted people who want to find another way to live. The hope is not only to offer protection to people in prostitution but also to make amends for the harms they have suffered by offering a path to a life of greater safety and dignity.

Those in favor of complete decriminalization argue that policing of prostitution does not protect the people whose bodies are being sold and in fact makes their lives more miserable and dangerous. The same goes for state regulation, as practiced in many countries worldwide and in the US state of Nevada. This is because those charged with policing prostitution often take advantage of their power by demanding that sex workers offer them free services as the price of their freedom. Considerable evidence supports this argument. A recent comprehensive review of reports from five continents concludes, "Police repression of sex workers increases the odds of HIV and other sexually transmitted infections, experiences of violence, financial extortion, condomless sex, and reduced access to justice."[14]

On the other hand, I and other radical feminists would argue, abolishing oppressive policing is necessary but not sufficient to address the harms of the sex trade. The absence of police is not the same as the presence of safety and certainly not the same as justice or repair. It is understandable that people who have been terribly exploited by police may wish to get rid of any role for the state with regard to the sex trade, but decriminalizing prostitution entirely still leaves the person sold for sex at the mercy of the john and the pimp. Studies of legalized prostitution in numerous countries report that, in fact, the expected harm reduction has not materialized; prostituted people are still mostly controlled by traffickers and exposed to violence, unprotected sex, and HIV at very high rates.[15] In New Zealand, for example, where prostitution was legalized in 2003 with high hopes of improving conditions for sex workers, a governmental commission report concluded five years later that these hopes had been disappointed. The majority of sex workers they interviewed felt that violence was an inevitable part of the sex trade and that the law could not do much about it.[16]

Twenty years of experience with the Swedish prostitution laws have resulted in a large body of evidence suggesting that the Nordic model is more effective than full decriminalization both in reducing prostitution overall and in reducing violence against prostituted people.[17] It is particularly noteworthy that in the two decades since the passage of these laws, no prostituted person has been murdered in Sweden, while in neighboring countries that legalize and regulate prostitution as sex work, such as Denmark,

Germany, and the Netherlands, murders and other forms of violence against sex workers have continued unabated.[18]

As of this writing, the New York State Legislature is considering two competing bills regarding prostitution, one advocating full decriminalization and the other, called the Equality Bill, advocating the Nordic model. Judge Camacho often travels to Albany to speak with state legislators in favor of the Equality Bill. "We're now at a point where I'm scared of losing twenty-five years' worth of work if full decriminalization passes," he says. "Prostitution is a multi-million-dollar business in New York State. Buyers are the key. If full decrim passes, demand will go through the roof, and trafficking will increase to meet demand. Organized crime will take over. They're already in, to the extent of local gangs, but once you get the international gangs, you'll never get rid of the corruption."[19]

Judge Camacho stayed in touch with Siobhan, the first young woman whom he remanded to care instead of jail. She dropped in to his court from time to time just to let him know that she was turning her life around. "Hey, Judge, I got a good job!" "Hey, Judge, I got my driver's license!" "Hey Judge, I'm in college now!" When he tells this story, people often say that he saved Siobhan's life. He doesn't see it that way. Rather, with characteristic humility, he asks, "Who do you think was most in need of being saved, a sixteen year old scared runaway who was forced into prostitution, or a forty three year old judge who for years had turned his back on the pain and suffering of our most vulnerable children? I think the truth is that she and I, in different ways, probably saved each other."[20] He says he still feels ashamed of his own participation in a system that punished and debased exploited young people and angry about the continuing ways commercial sexual exploitation is socially condoned, but he also feels redeemed by the ways he has been able to make a difference in so many young lives. "I believe there is a light inside of every one of us," he says. "If you suffer so much over and over, that light goes out. I can see the dead eyes when the light has gone out, and I can see it when that light comes back."[21] In a career devoted to justice, he has come to believe that repairing the relationship between the crime victim and the implicated bystanders in her moral community can be healing for all.

Survivors' Justice

Restitution, in sum, can take many forms. There are many different ways that survivors can be "made whole" by their communities, and direct financial compensation to individuals for their injuries is only one of them. Of equal importance to many survivors is evidence of active community efforts to change the systems that have allowed violence and exploitation to flourish. That may mean requiring offenders to give back to victims by paying for crisis services that promote healing. It may mean removing predators from positions of authority in the workplace and changing the workplace culture so that their behavior is no longer so passively tolerated. It may mean bringing victim advocates into courtrooms or legal services into women's homes. It may mean changing the culture of machismo within police departments. It may mean developing specialized courts to assist victims of sex trafficking or changing the laws that dehumanize them and treat them as criminals. All these innovative forms of repair can represent survivors' justice.

8

REHABILITATION

I don't want to be some dumb-ass who hurts people anymore.

—"Jerry," graduate of a sex offender treatment program[1]

If locking up perpetrators is not the metric of justice, then what can be done to deter them from repeating their crimes and to protect public safety? Survivors often see rehabilitation as a better form of justice than punishment. Many say that if they had their way, they would wish for the people who harmed them to be somehow induced to repent and reform. But the sad truth is, although the justice system has invested so heavily in prisons, it has never made even a remotely comparable investment in rehabilitation. As a result, we know little about what it would actually take to bring perpetrators to relinquish violence and feel genuine remorse for their crimes. We don't know how to instill empathy or a feeling of common humanity in those who lack it. Since the great majority of offenders never come to any form of public attention, we lack the most basic information about them: who they are, what led them to their crimes, and what might lead them to a moral awakening that would allow their safe reintegration into their communities.

One very popular idea, frequently repeated both in the media and in professional circles, is that most perpetrators of sexual violence must have been abused themselves as children. Is this true? The most honest answer would be that we don't know for sure, but probably not. It is comforting to have an explanation of some sort, but the evidence is very thin once one looks carefully. For example, most studies of sex offenders are conducted with prisoners who have been convicted of sex crimes. True, these studies tend to find many with histories of childhood abuse.[2] But this is true of imprisoned people in general; in fact, incarcerated women, most of whom are in prison for nonviolent offenses, have rates of childhood victimization that are as high or even higher than those for incarcerated male sex offenders.[3] So studies of prisoners don't tell us anything specific about sex offenders; they just tell us about the misfortunes of people who end up in prison.

Moreover, since most sex crimes are never reported, and since the vast majority of men who commit these crimes are never brought to justice, one cannot draw any inferences about the majority of offenders simply from studying the few who are caught and convicted. For one extreme example, a recent study of convicted sex offenders in Minnesota reported that over 80 percent were Black men.[4] Does this mean that most sex offenders are Black? Of course not! Rather, it reflects the enormous racial disparities in our country's criminal justice system. Too often, Black men are tried, convicted, and sentenced to long prison terms for the same crimes that white men commit with no legal consequences whatsoever. The pernicious racist and patriarchal fantasy of Black assault on "pure white womanhood," a fantasy that incited lynch mobs in the past, still animates the public today. In those rare instances when a Black stranger attacks a white woman, the state spares no energy in hunting down and punishing the offender. But in reality most rapists are not strangers to their victims; they are acquaintances, bosses, dates, boyfriends, or husbands. Most men who rape white women in the United States are white. As we saw in Chapter 3, their odds of being caught or punished are close to nil.

Perpetrators who have *not* been caught do not generally volunteer to be research subjects, so we know almost nothing about them. Finding out more about the perpetrators in our midst has not exactly been a public health research priority, so at present we don't have answers even to the most basic questions of epidemiology. We don't know what percentage of men in the general population commit rape or how these men differ from those who do not. In the rare confidential studies that have been conducted with perpetrators at large in the community, the researchers have been left scratching their heads for an explanation. By and large, these perpetrators do *not* report childhood abuse; nor do they meet criteria for any psychiatric diagnosis. Like others who commit crimes sanctioned by tyrannical regimes, they look frighteningly normal.[5]

Journalist Rachel Louise Snyder, who spent a good deal of time observing treatment groups for men who batter, remarked that they seemed like regular guys whom she might enjoy having a beer with. "We look for talons and tails," she wrote, "but find instead charm and affability. It's how abusers attract victims in the first place."[6] One might consider perpetrators of gender-based violence for the most part as opportunistic offenders; that is, they would be much less likely to commit these crimes if they didn't have very good reason to believe that they would never be held accountable.

We do know that many perpetrators of gender-based violence embrace highly misogynistic attitudes that rationalize, even glorify, their behavior. As one frat brother at the University of Southern California said of women, in his weekly personal newsletter on how to be a "cocksman," "They aren't actual people like us men."[7] When promoted among peers, such attitudes can be expected to translate into misogynistic practices, up to and including crimes of violence. Recent confidential studies of men who commit sexual assaults on college campuses report that even at this youthful age, many have already developed a pattern of repeat offenses.[8]

The nurse Sarah Johnson, whom we met in Chapter 5, a survivor of rape by a fellow student in high school, described the impact of discovering that she was not the first of the boy's victims:

> The detective told me he knew what happened—he'd done this to between five and ten other girls. There had been complaints, but none of them would press charges. He said, "Sarah, you'd be helping many girls if you did." When he was arrested, his father called us and said, "How much do you want? Can't we just

work this out and forget it?" My dad hung up on him. His parents have always given him everything, always bailed him out. I don't know if that kind of person can be rehabilitated.

In this case, the fact that the father had repeatedly covered up for his son allowed the boy to get away with multiple offenses. And certainly, conventional wisdom holds that repeat offenders are much harder to rehabilitate than those who face justice the first time they commit crimes.

Reverend Anne Marie Hunter, whom we also met in Chapter 5, expressed similar skepticism about rehabilitation of batterers, given how society enables their behavior. She knew firsthand how commonly the justice system failed to enforce court orders for protection or child support and how commonly the clergy counseled women to submit to abuse in order to fulfill their marriage vows and keep the family together. She thought that because batterers live by the rules of tyranny, the only motivation for them to change might be a forceful mandate from a higher (male) authority. Regarding her ex-husband, she was sure that no amount of reproach from women would matter at all to him. The only thing that might make a difference, she imagined, would be "if his father, who treated his mother the same way, had a change of heart and came to him and told him he should do the same, or if his boss told him that what he did was unacceptable, or if a religious leader forcefully denounced him to his face or from the pulpit."

Most existing rehabilitation programs, including those of restorative justice (RJ), do in fact rely on the higher authority of the criminal courts and the ultimate threat of punishment to ensure the offender's compliance. Voluntary participation in such programs is unusual. Since, in fact, most offenders never see the inside of a courtroom, what we know about existing rehabilitation programs tells us very little about what might be effective for the majority of offenders who enjoy impunity. Moreover, because so little has been invested in offender rehabilitation, few treatment programs have gathered enough follow-up data to report anything more than anecdotal evidence of their effectiveness. Nevertheless, we do have a few models of survivor-centered rehabilitation, which I review in this chapter as a way to help us look toward how we might begin to develop this aspect of survivors' justice.

Programs for Intimate Partner Violence

The most widely implemented and well-documented batterer treatment program, known as the Duluth Model, comes from the grassroots feminist organization in Minnesota that created the "Violence Wheel" in the 1980s. The mission of the organization, now known as Domestic Abuse Intervention Programs, is to end violence against women, nothing less. Its website states, "We give voice to diverse women who are battered, by translating their experiences into innovative programs and institutional changes that centralize victim safety. We partner with communities worldwide to inspire the social and political will to eliminate violence against women and their families."[9]

Unlike "anger management," with which it is often confused, the Duluth Model is based on an understanding of domestic violence not as an outlet for a troubled man needing to vent his anger, nor as a loss of control, but rather as a choice, a calculated means of asserting dominance and control over another human being. Program advocates point out, quite correctly, that most men who assault their partners are perfectly capable of controlling their anger around their bosses or their coworkers. Abusers exercise their violence only on those who have less power. The Duluth rehabilitation model requires the coordinated power of police, prosecutors, and court intervention to protect battered women and to mandate batterers into outpatient treatment. It is an explicitly victim-centered model that calls on the justice system to define the safety and well-being of victims, rather than conviction of perpetrators, as its primary measure of success.

This is the kind of certified batterer intervention program that Reverend Hunter references in her sermon (quoted in Chapter 5). Offenders are treated in groups, where they are taught about issues of gender, relationships, power, and control. They are given the opportunity to process their feelings about these matters and to call one another out on their rationalizations and excuses, which they recognize only too well. Studies with programs following this model offer some hopeful outcomes that show decreases in reports of violence and improved self-respect for survivors after one to two years.[10]

Treatment programs of this type have also faced harsh criticism claiming that they are not sufficiently "evidence-based" or, more crudely, that they don't work. Much of this criticism comes from mental health professionals who focus on the individual pathology of offenders and reject a social analysis (especially a feminist analysis) of battering. It also comes from policymakers, who quite understandably want concrete evidence that any funding for such programs will be well spent.

In a thoughtful review, Edward Gondolf, a longtime researcher in this field, explains why a biomedical research model is inappropriate for evaluating this kind of program. The so-called gold standard of medical research is the randomized, controlled trial. Doses and protocols for an experimental drug are standardized so that every patient gets exactly the same treatment, patients are randomly assigned to different treatment conditions, and both patients and researchers are "blinded," so they don't know who is getting which treatment until after all the results are recorded. This degree of rigor for "evidence-based" treatment outcome research is simply impossible when studying the effectiveness of psychosocial interventions.

As Gondolf explains, batterer treatment programs are complex organizations with many moving parts that have to work together well to balance both mental health and criminal justice objectives. Many variables also have to be taken into account: who is referred for treatment, for instance, and for how long and with what kind of follow-up. Regarding the treatment population, clearly not all batterers are the same. Some will probably respond well to a variety of different treatments; some have special needs that need to be taken into account; some are true sociopaths and probably unreachable by any known treatment method. Programs will have better outcomes if a good risk-screening method is in place for referrals so that the most dangerous offenders are not sent to outpatient treatment.

Then there is the matter of collaboration between the treatment programs and the courts. In some programs, judges and probation officers are actively engaged in regular follow-up, so that offenders who drop out of treatment face reliable consequences; those programs will have lower dropout rates and better outcomes than programs where court supervision is laxer. Consequences do not need to be severe to deter further violence, but they do need to be swift and predictable. This means changing the current practices in many courts, where consequences for violating court orders may be severe in theory, but oversight is sporadic, so that in fact the chances of getting away with new infractions are good.

Gondolf argues that neither probation alone nor treatment alone has proven effective; rather, the *combination* of batterer treatment programs with active court oversight makes for effectiveness in reducing recidivism. As we saw in Chapter 7, creating true safety for survivors often requires new forms of cooperation between systems of justice and mental health. He concludes that existing data are encouraging enough to support continued implementation of programs that follow the basic Duluth Model, with additional attention to issues like substance abuse and cultural sensitivity to different ethnic groups. The main expansion he recommends is strengthening the personal connections between program staff and the community agencies that represent the ecosystem of domestic violence response, so that clinicians have good, first-name-basis working relationships with victim advocates, police, prosecutors, probation officers, and judges.[11]

Note that this is the same kind of community building that Judge Camacho recommended in Chapter 7. In other words, changing violent behavior that has been so widespread, so endemic, and for so long ignored as a victim's private misfortune requires community organizing to develop a new, complex, and well-coordinated social intervention system. It means, in effect, building an alternative moral community, one that no longer condones or excuses the violence and turns a blind eye but instead fully accepts responsibility for ending it.

In Atlanta, a group called Men Stopping Violence (MSV) has developed its Community Accountability Model, which illustrates one way of building that alternative moral community. It begins with a six-month Batterer Intervention Program but moves well beyond this to engage in much broader culture change. Rather than focusing on the individual pathology of offenders, MSV diagnoses violence against women as an inevitable consequence of patriarchal systems that define manhood as dominance and expands its programming from batterer intervention to community action. It argues that batterer intervention programs alone, while a necessary first step, will never be sufficient to address the problem, first, because most domestic violence is never reported to law enforcement and, second, because the burden of arrest and court-mandated treatment falls disproportionately on working-class men and men of color, while men with the most privilege are never held to account. Most importantly, MSV conceives of domestic violence as a problem for the entire social system that effectively condones it rather than simply for the individuals involved.

Some of the innovations developed by MSV include a requirement that offenders invite other men from their communities—friends, family members, coworkers, pastors, and fraternity brothers—to join their batterers' educational groups and take part in their discussions. These men become "accountability partners" for the offenders. MSV recognizes that sustaining change once the groups end will be difficult for individual offenders in the face of patriarchal community norms. Accountability partners become an alternative support system, certainly less coercive and potentially more effective than probation in the long term.

Equally important is the effect of the educational programs on the accountability partners themselves. These men may never have been violent, but they, too, can question their male supremacist beliefs, and they, too, can become agents of change. Offenders and their accountability partners who have completed the six-month educational program can themselves become community educators. MSV sponsors an initiative called the Community Restoration Program, which both serves as an ongoing support group for graduates and engages them in activities like mentoring young people and speaking to community groups about violence against women.[12] As offenders become catalysts for social change, they have the opportunity not only for personal rehabilitation but also for making amends in a larger sense, by giving back to their communities. This model embodies the reparative principles of survivors' justice.

Sex Offender Treatment

We have noted that very few sex offenders seek rehabilitation voluntarily. Why should they, as long as they can get away with these assaults? Therefore, most existing treatment models for this group have been developed for incarcerated men or those who have been court ordered into outpatient therapy after serving a prison sentence. The men who have been sentenced for these crimes are such a small fraction of the general offender population that treatments developed for them may have very little relevance for the undetected majority of offenders who never face any legal consequences for their actions. To date, the evidence for the effectiveness of sex offender treatment has been equivocal. In a recent review, psychologists Jill Stinson and Judith Becker, who are experts in this field, critique previous treatment models and conclude that most well-controlled studies report "weak, mixed, or null" results in reducing recidivism.

Stinson and Becker propose a new "evidence-based" treatment model that was developed in two inpatient forensic mental health facilities and one facility for sexually violent predators. As one might expect, these incarcerated patients are much more obviously and severely impaired than the vast majority of offenders at large in the community. Their detailed treatment manual, called Safe Offender Strategies (SOS), prescribes weekly psychotherapy sessions, usually in a group, for a recommended average duration of four years. They recognize that treating offenders requires a very special kind of therapist, a person who can feel empathy for these patients despite knowing how much harm they have done to others, and who can accept them as they are, suspending judgment, while at the same time trying to engage them in a desire to change.

A pilot study of SOS shows that after two years of treatment, inmates who attend sessions regularly have fewer aggressive outbursts, repeat offenses (which do occur, even in the confines of the facility), suicidal behaviors, and episodes of seclusion or restraint compared with those whose attendance is irregular.[13] These results might seem promising at first glance, but actually we already know that motivation is one of the best predictors of treatment outcome, so this pilot study really just adds to the evidence that patients who show up do better in treatment. The study doesn't tell us a lot about the effectiveness of this specific form of treatment. Though this new manual is well thought out, the SOS model has yet to demonstrate good results with patients who are eventually released back into the community, let alone with a more general outpatient population of offenders. So it seems a bit premature to call it "evidence based." But this has become something of a buzzword to impress funders, both in academia and in government policy circles.

Some of the challenges and complexities that prison-based offender treatments face can be illustrated by the story of Wynona Ward, the founder of Have Justice—Will Travel, whom we met in Chapter 7. As a young girl she was close to her older brother, Richard. He taught her to hunt (for food, not sport) when she was seven and he was nine, and he often tried to intervene, even at that young age, when their father was beating their mother, knowing he would take a beating as well. So she saw her brother as caring and courageous. But Richard, as the only son, was also the "inheritor" of their father's "kingdom," as Ward put it, and though he spared his pal Wynona, he sexually abused their two younger sisters. The girls never talked about this when they were children, but years later, when Ward learned that Richard had begun abusing their six-year-old niece, she decided that the cycle of violence in this family had to stop. She and her two younger sisters banded together and reported the crime. Richard was arrested, tried, convicted, and sentenced to prison.

Like so many other court cases involving child abuse, this one divided the family. Their father, mother, and oldest sister adamantly insisted that Richard was not guilty and encouraged him to remain steadfast in his denial throughout multiple appeals. The two halves of the family did not speak to one another for years. At the trial, Ward recounted, the prosecutor asked her an unexpected question: "Do you love your brother?" "I knew my brother when he was a good little boy," she replied. "My parents have made a monster of him." She also recognized that though she could see Richard's humanity, her niece could not. Ward was not afraid of Richard, still cared for him, and wanted him to get help; her niece, however, was still in terror of Richard and just wanted him to be locked up forever.

Richard remained in complete denial until the death of their father. Only then was he ready to admit what he had done and enter a prison treatment program for sex offenders. In other words, even the most coercive power of the state was not sufficient to break the coercive control exercised over this offender, who was also a victim, by his father. Only the death of his father released him.

Once Richard admitted abusing his niece and began offender treatment, Ward began visiting him in prison. She thought the program was good for him. "They worked with him for a year to get him to admit all the abuse," she reported. "He had written his autobiography. He knew how to talk the talk. I was hopeful. He was coming along. But it still wasn't really his fault. It was still the victim's fault. He had no empathy for the victim. That's the last thing to come."

Because of Richard's continued lack of empathy, despite his progress, Ward and her sisters did not feel that he was ready to be released from prison, and they opposed a recommendation for parole. Richard died in prison. "I really wanted my brother to get out of prison, to enjoy nature, growing things," Ward said. "The treatment program was wonderful. I've seen research that says it's one of the best in the country. But even with that, I was scared to death that he would abuse someone else again." In other words, even the best prison-based programs are still very much a work in progress. Particularly with repeat offenders, treatment offers no reliable assurance that prisoners can be returned safely to the community.

One small community-based program for lower-level sex offenders has frequently been cited as a promising model because it does have some published outcome data. This was a demonstration project called RESTORE, developed by psychology professor Mary Koss, based on a feminist understanding of restorative justice principles.[14] The program relied on the criminal justice system to refer selected offenders for possible RJ conferencing. Over the course of four years, the local district attorney's office in Tucson, Arizona, referred sixty-six men to the program, ruling out cases involving a high degree of violence or repeat offenders. The format was to seek consent first from the "victim/survivors." The program reached out to them and was able to contact fifty-seven people, of whom thirty-nine (about two-thirds) agreed to participate. The program then reached out to the thirty-nine "responsible persons," of whom twenty-two men (about half) consented and "acknowledged responsibility" for the crime. Those accused of misdemeanors were more likely to agree than those accused of felonies. Thus, in the end, one-third of the referred cases were screened into the treatment program.

In exchange for the admission of responsibility (which avoided the word "guilty"), the threat of a criminal trial was suspended, though it remained in force for those who did not follow through. Technically, this would be called a "diversion" program. Twenty cases proceeded to a carefully prepared and supervised RJ conference, witnessed by family and friends of both the victim and the perpetrator. In these meetings, victims and witnesses had the opportunity to tell their stories and express their wishes, perpetrators listened, and a plan of redress was developed. After a year of follow-up monitoring, sixteen perpetrators (or "responsible persons," in the language of the program) had completed all aspects of their redress plans.

This attrition rate might seem to compare favorably with that of the conventional justice system, where conviction rates are less than 5 percent. Still, fewer than one in four cases diverted to RESTORE actually led to successful completion of a plan for repair, and this despite the fact that the program was restricted to the less obviously dangerous cases. Clearly, even the most innovative models for repairing the harm of sex crimes and rehabilitating offenders are much in need of further development.

The RJ goals of the RESTORE program, in particular the emphasis on apology, were not completely aligned with those of the survivors who participated. Many of the twenty "responsible persons" apologized during the course of their conferences. The survivors, however, like the people whom I interviewed, were divided about whether they even wished for an apology, and many did not trust that an apology could ever be sincere. For the majority, healing the relationship with the perpetrator was not their primary goal; rather, they wished "to make the responsible person accountable" and "to make sure that the responsible person doesn't do what he did to anyone else." Like the people whom I interviewed, they stated that their primary objective was prevention of future harm. And even though both the victims and the perpetrators who went through this program mainly expressed satisfaction with the outcome, we have no follow-up data on whether the main objective of rehabilitation, reduced recidivism, was accomplished.

Giving Back to Victims and the Community

Because sex offender treatment reaches such a limited population, any innovation that expands its availability might form a promising basis for future outcome research. A recently developed model that potentially addresses the needs of both offenders and victims is called vicarious restorative justice (VRJ). In this form of treatment, survivors of sexual violence are invited to attend therapy groups for men who are court mandated to sex offender treatment, so that the men can hear directly from survivors about the impact of the kind of crimes that they have committed and can hopefully show the survivors some genuine respect. One advantage of this model is that survivors have a chance to meet with men who have said they are ready to take responsibility for their actions and express remorse. This type of encounter greatly enlarges the possibilities for a restorative approach. Survivors can choose to participate when the timing is right for them, regardless of whether the particular men who harmed them are willing to admit responsibility, then or ever. Some survivors never want to see those particular men in any case. For offenders, meeting with survivors can enhance their understanding of the consequences of their actions, and listening to survivors can serve as a kind of amends.

Criminologist Alissa Ackerman, a professor and a rape survivor who recently coauthored a book about vicarious restorative justice, tells the following story: At an unsupervised beach party in Florida, when she was sixteen, she agreed to go for a walk on the beach with a boy she barely knew, a friend of friends. Apparently he thought that going for a walk meant that she was consenting to sex. When she said no, explaining, "I like girls," the boy attacked her. He told her this was her punishment for refusing him and for being a "disgusting dyke."

Since coming out as queer, she had been alienated from her parents, who disapproved. Feeling alone and unsupported, she told no one, and her life spiraled out of control. She went from being a straight-A student and star athlete to flunking out of school. No one seemed to notice, and she got no help until age nineteen, when she met her current partner, a woman whom she credits with believing in her and saving her life. Before the assault she had wanted to major in biology, but afterward she went back to school to study why people become violent. Even during the assault, she said, she remembers thinking, "What happened to you that made you think what you're doing is okay?" In a criminology class, she learned about the effects of sexual violence and for the first time realized that she wasn't alone. As she gained her doctorate, she slowly developed her survivor mission. Now she says, "My work is a calling. It is why I am on this earth."

I asked her what she would want from the man who had raped her, and she listed the following: (1) an acknowledgment of what he did, (2) an explanation of why he did it, and (3) reparations. This meant first of all repayment of all the money she had spent on her mental health care over the years. "Making amends is not just 'I'm sorry,'" she explained. "It's something you do over a long time." In addition to her own personal reparations, she would want the rapist to give back to the community, in the form of public testimony. "I would like nothing more than to stand in a room with him and have him say 'I did this,' and look me in the eye," she said, "perhaps in a high school talking to sixteen-year-olds about the effects of sexual violence." This is the kind of preventive education that she imagines would have been most helpful to her during her own adolescence: "People talking to young kids about body autonomy and sex in general, and what consent means, that it's never okay to violate those boundaries."

Dr. Ackerman also talked about what she wanted from the bystanders, the people who saw that she was in trouble when she was a teenager and failed to intervene. "I needed somebody to ask if I was okay," she said. "Anybody who knew anything about me knew I wasn't okay. That's where more of my anger lies now. What I don't understand is how you can watch it happen and do nothing." Asked how bystanders should be held accountable, she cited the familiar triad of acknowledgment, apology, and amends. She reported that recently this had occurred in a meeting with her parents after they attended synagogue together. "My mother acknowledged and apologized," she said. "We're much closer now."

Years after the assault, Dr. Ackerman disclosed her secret to a professor, Dr. Jill Levenson, who had been a mentor to her and had become a colleague and friend. Dr. Levenson invited her to meet with men in a sex offender treatment group she had been conducting. "It was life changing," Ackerman reported. "I felt safe. I shared details of my victimization. They listened. They understood. They said 'you didn't do anything wrong.'" By speaking her truth to the group, she gained the acknowledgment and vindication that she could never get from the man who raped her. She also reported that it was a great relief to see the men in the group just as fallible human beings. Here I note that many of the survivors I interviewed have also stressed the importance for their *own* mental health of being able to recognize the humanity of their abusers. As long as they feel that these men are "monsters," they continue to fear them and see them as having almost supernatural powers. Through participation in the group, Dr. Ackerman realized, to her astonishment, that these men were actually afraid of her. "They are so afraid of women's justified anger, the names they're going to be called. They're so ashamed. They can't face it," she said.

The men in the group asked Dr. Ackerman what she would say to the man who raped her if he were in the group. She answered that although she forgave him a long time ago, she would want him to know how the rape has impacted every aspect of her life. "I have a beautiful life, now," she said, "but I still have PTSD. I can't wrestle on the floor with my kids. If my child jumps on me, I can't feel my body." Here it is important to note that although Dr. Ackerman had chosen unilaterally to forgive her assailant, she did not think to forgive any of the offenders whom she met in the group. This is because the choice to forgive a particular offender belongs only to the person whom he has harmed. No one else has the prerogative to forgive on the victim's behalf.

As they discussed this powerful group experience, Drs. Ackerman and Levenson came to understand that they had invented a new form of restorative justice, and they began collaborating to implement similar groups. Recently, they published a slim volume describing their model.[15] Their arguments are mainly based on case studies; like most professionals who work with offenders, they do not have any formal outcome data to present. But this is the state of the field at present.

Like many other advocates for restorative justice, Dr. Ackerman maintains that VRJ is more a set of principles than specific practices, and therefore the concept lends itself to creative adaptation in a variety of settings outside the framework of the criminal justice system. For example, I asked her whether she thought that VRJ principles could be useful in responding to sexual violence in a college campus setting. She replied that she did think so, as long as some "reporters" and "respondents" were willing to take part. Young offenders who accepted responsibility would be more actively included in campus life rather than excluded. They would be asked not only to participate in their own remedial education program but also to make amends to the campus community by taking part in preventive education for other students.

"I teach a course on sex crimes at my university," Dr. Ackerman said. "I could see a part of VRJ accountability requiring a student to be in the class for the semester, with the understanding that, from day one, they will publicly own that they committed rape and that this is part of their process of making amends." In other words, through public acknowledgment and participation in an educational endeavor, young offenders would have the opportunity to expiate their guilt and to promote both their own healing and the health of the wider community. This concept is similar to the community accountability model developed by Men Stopping Violence. It begins with treatment for individual offenders but does not end there; rather, it expands into education for social change, giving offenders a way to deepen their own understanding of the harm they have done and to contribute to community repair.

In sum, because our system of justice has invested so much in punishing and incapacitating offenders and so little in understanding and rehabilitating them, at present this aspect of survivors' justice remains visionary. That does not mean that it is impossible, but it does mean that developing and implementing a program of rehabilitation on the vast scale required would necessitate lots of research and a massive reform of our concepts and practices of justice. Crimes of dominance and subordination would need to be approached as a matter of public health as well as public safety, with prevention as a primary goal. Rather than focusing on punishing the few individual offenders who were caught, the justice system would need to focus on changing the social and cultural factors that increase risk of offending, with the goal not only of rehabilitating those who have already offended but also of preventing the occurrence of these offenses in the first place.

As Dr. Ackerman suggests, one promising site for experimentation with these visionary ideas about rehabilitation and prevention might be a class on sex crimes at her university. We turn now to a discussion of the college campus as a potential site for developing creative new ideas about survivors' justice.

9

PREVENTION

If we want to teach our children to be decent human beings who respect others and themselves, we have to tackle notions of masculinity and femininity. And patriarchy. No, don't run away. We really do.

—Sohaila Abdulali, *What We Talk About When We Talk About Rape*[1]

In Chapter 4, we told the story of Lybia Rivera, who suffered sexual harassment when she was a graduate student at Harvard and was eventually driven to leave without completing her degree. Sadly, the hostile climate that she encountered is not at all unusual on college campuses. College students are at the age of highest risk for sexual assault, and on many campuses, sexual assault, like hazing, has the status of a traditional initiation rite, being implicitly tolerated if not openly celebrated. It should be noted that this level of risk does not apply to college students alone. In fact, less privileged young people in the same age group are at even greater risk. Studies of sexual assault in the military and in jobs like food service and agricultural work make this abundantly clear. But the college campus offers something unique: a relatively contained environment for conducting new experiments with prevention. If the campus can be a place of danger, it can also be a place of intellectual and political awakening.

In recent years, survivors of campus sexual assault and harassment have named the hostile campus climate as "rape culture" and demanded that it be changed. With its mission to promote free inquiry and innovation, the college campus can be a model for an alternative moral community, a place to envision new customs and rules for a culture of sexual mutuality and respect, and a potential laboratory for survivors' justice.

Title IX of the amended Civil Rights Act of 1972 prohibits sex discrimination in educational institutions. In recent years, feminist activists have advanced the argument that the entrenched rape culture on college campuses deprives women of equal access to education and therefore constitutes a form of sex discrimination and that colleges have an affirmative duty to put an end to it. During the Barack Obama administration, the Department of Education took an active stance on this issue, developing new guidelines for institutional responses to sexual assault and conducting thorough investigations into Title IX complaints. Many colleges and universities (including my own) were found to be in violation of Title IX, and some schools entered into consent decrees requiring them to develop new ways to educate the student body, to protect survivors, and to hold perpetrators accountable. The White House also sponsored an initiative called "It's on Us," which encourages bystanders, especially young men, to intervene on behalf of victims when they witness sexually aggressive behavior. This initiative, which recognizes the all-important role of bystanders, has the potential to change the culture, for if bystanders are no longer passively complicit, then the perpetrator, not the victim, faces the prospect of social isolation and shame.

Studies of campus rapists cite the powerful enabling role of peer support. Members of all-male fraternal or athletic groups are far more likely than other young men to commit rape.[2] Anthropologist Peggy Sanday describes a fraternity culture that ritualizes gang rape as a form of male bonding and inculcates the belief that sexual exploitation is a normal male entitlement. Prestigious, highly selective all-male groups like fraternities often have elaborate traditions in which new recruits first learn the methods of dominance and subordination by submitting to harsh initiation rites themselves. Later, when they have been admitted to the group, they gain the privilege of practicing these same methods on women (and subordinate men). Noting that the word "victim" derives from the Latin word for a beast chosen for sacrifice in a religious ritual, Professor Sanday writes, "The god being served in rituals of group sex is brotherhood."

Investigating two fraternities where "trains" (i.e., gang rape) were customary, Professor Sanday found secret rituals that symbolized a "covenant of power," handed down from one generation to the next and practiced in all chapters. Initiation practices included chants of "Die, pussies, die," stripping, beating, mock execution, and, of course, rapid ingestion of toxic amounts of alcohol, followed by having to clean up vomit and excrement. In these rites, the pledge undergoes the symbolic death of his vulnerable boyhood self, bonded to mother, and is reborn with a powerful manhood self, bonded to the brotherhood.[3] Initiates in some brotherhoods, particularly athletic teams, may also be subjected to group sexual assault, as in the practice of "brooming" (i.e., anal rape with an object).[4] One might add that literal, not symbolic, deaths, usually from alcohol poisoning or related accidents, do sometimes occur during hazing. The individuals and organizations responsible are very rarely held to account in any serious way.

Legal scholar Diane Rosenfeld, who directs the Gender Violence Program at Harvard Law School, describes a fraternity party practice of premeditated "target rape," in which women are invited based on their relative inexperience and vulnerability, and sexual assaults are carefully planned before the party and celebrated by the group afterward.[5] Any attempt to change the attitudes and behavior of the perpetrators, then, must also address the deeply entrenched male supremacist attitudes and customs of their peer group. Imagine the courage it requires at present for a young man to speak up against sexist behavior. In fact, his is the voice of the majority; the good news is that, as far as we know, most young men do *not* sexually harass or assault women.[6] But, by and large, the majority have long been passive or implicated bystanders.

The Tripod: Leg One

In her prescription for effective responses to rape on college campuses, Professor Rosenfeld describes a "tripod" of preventive education, victim support, and consistent discipline of perpetrators. She proposes that student trust in the campus community requires all three, just as a tripod needs three legs to stand on. If one considers sexual assault from a public health perspective, the educational component of the tripod would be considered primary prevention: stopping assaults before they happen. The other two components would be considered secondary prevention: mitigating the harm of assaults after they happen and disciplining offenders effectively so that they will not reoffend and so others may be deterred from offending.

Much creative work has been done on preventive education, as might be expected in educational settings. The most basic level involves simply naming the problem, informing students of their rights, and explaining the options available to them if they are subjected to sexual harassment and assault. It has become clear, however, that sexual assault prevention is not simply a matter of checking off a box, such as providing a required lecture during freshman orientation or distributing a handbook of student rights and responsibilities. Changing rape culture requires ongoing engagement of all members of the campus community. It requires interpersonal dialogues in small groups, sex education focused on mutuality and consent, changes in social drinking and party customs, and practice for bystanders in new ways of responding to common risky scenarios. Even physical changes in the campus environment can serve a primary preventive function.

In a recent workshop on responses to sexual misconduct on college campuses, Professors Shamus Khan, from Princeton University, and Jennifer Hirsch, from Columbia University, gave a keynote lecture titled "Sexual Citizens: A Landmark Study of Sex, Power, and Assault on Campus."[7] This is also the title of their 2020 book. Conceptually, they view college campuses as a "social ecosystem," identifying physical spaces, alcohol, peer groups, and cultural norms as factors that influence the incidence of sexual assault and targeting those factors in their efforts at primary prevention.

Starting with an analysis of the way that control of physical spaces expresses inequalities of power, Professors Khan and Hirsch consider some practical ways these spaces could be utilized differently. For example, they note that young people need places to go after parties besides dorm rooms, where the beds are the only places to sit, and they suggest that keeping a cafeteria open all night reduces opportunities for sexual assault. They wonder why seniors and athletes get the best dorm rooms and suggest instead that these rooms might be assigned to entering freshmen from the most disadvantaged families, inverting the customary power hierarchy. They also recognize that most college students don't live on residential campuses but suggest that community colleges, too, can conduct "space audits" to promote what they call a "geography of equality."

Then there is the matter of sex education. Professors Khan and Hirsch recognize both the potential power of sex education and the fact that most entering college students, even if otherwise very well educated, are remarkably ignorant in this domain. With rare exceptions, the students' formal sex education in secondary school has been either nonexistent or focused on abstinence, a type of sex ed shown to be utterly ineffective. Their informal sex education has come mainly from pornography, in which domination is what makes sex sexy. Young men learn to be sexually aroused and fulfilled by fantasies of imposing their power on women, and young women learn they are supposed to be aroused and fulfilled by submission.

In fact, being dominated does not give most women pleasure, but many learn to fake it because they have been socialized into the belief that men are entitled to sex, especially once aroused, and women are obliged to give men what they want. And faking it works well enough, since many young men do not bother to inquire about their partners' desires, either because they don't really care or because they have been socialized into the belief that whatever satisfies them must satisfy their partners as well. Professor Hirsch remarked that she couldn't even count the number of young women who had confided that they felt trapped in a dating situation and "gave him a blow job just to get out of there." It's usually unclear exactly what these young women were afraid of—whether it was actually being forced into intercourse, or perhaps making their dates angry, or just failing to satisfy them—but clearly they were intimidated. Nevertheless, they generally thought of these encounters as consensual, and no doubt their dates did as well.

In contrast, the concept of sexual citizenship suggests that young people have equal rights to "sexual self-determination," meaning the right to say yes when they feel authentic desire and to say no when they do not. Of course, this is what women have been saying, indeed chanting, for years now, in Take Back the Night demonstrations against sexual violence: "Yes means yes! No means no! However we dress! Wherever we go!" Professor Hirsch notes that young women who are lucky enough to have had "practice-based" sex education, where they have actually practiced saying no in simulated dating situations, are half as likely to be raped in college.[8]

For young men, sexual citizenship means learning concepts of mutuality and consent in sexual relations. This in turn means *un*learning the sexual ideology of pornography. The basic pornographic fantasy is that women secretly long to be overpowered and "possessed" by domineering men. Porn inculcates the belief that the more women protest, the more they really, really want it. As Yale fraternity pledges famously chanted beneath a women's freshman dormitory, in rebuttal to Take Back the Night, "No means yes! Yes means anal!" One might consider this chant simply vulgar sexist provocation, which of course it was, but unfortunately it also expresses crude fantasies that are widely shared.

Sex educator Peggy Orenstein writes that when talking with boys, she never asks *whether* they've seen porn but rather *when* they first saw it. Most began using porn around puberty, and most continue to use it. She minces no words about what pornographic images portray. "The free content most readily available to minors tends to show sex as something men do *to* women rather than *with* women [and] often portrays female pleasure as a performance for male satisfaction." She adds that Black women are frequently portrayed as "loose" and therefore legitimate targets of aggression, and Black men are portrayed as dangerous sex fiends. "In other words," she writes, "teenagers are being served a heaping helping of racism with their eroticized misogyny."[9]

Legal scholar Catharine MacKinnon describes the intrinsic violence of porn in even starker terms. "In pornography," she writes, in her inimitable blunt language, "there it is, all in one place, all the abuses that women had to struggle so long to articulate, all the *unspeakable* abuse: the rape, the battery, the sexual harassment, prostitution, and sexual abuse of children. Only in the pornography, it is called something else: sex, sex, sex, sex and sex, respectively."[10]

In order to counter the eroticized misogyny of porn, sex education must expand, from the issue of consent in sexual relations to a wider understanding of how male dominance and female subordination shape the most basic concepts of masculine and feminine. Some model campus programs have gone about this in promising ways. At Northwestern University, for example, psychologist Saed Deryck Hill directs the Masculinity, Allyship, Reflection, Solidarity (MARS) program, which educates volunteer peer counselors. In a six-week course, young men have group discussions on gender-based socialization and are asked to keep daily journals, with prompts focusing on emotional reactions. "We have to give them a list of emotions, because initially they don't know how to name feelings," says Dr. Hill. "If you ask them what they're feeling, they say 'Okay,' or 'fine.' By week three or four, they become more expressive, and in discussions they realize just how restricted their masculinity has been." He prefers the term "restrictive masculinity" to the more pejorative "toxic masculinity."

Peer educators at Northwestern also participate in a consciousness-raising exercise called the "Man Box." Dr. Hill asks the young men to create a list of words or phrases describing what it means to be a man. "It's always the same list," he says. He writes the words on a blackboard: "tough," "stoical," "likes sports," "drinks beer," "eats meat," "has sex with a lot of women," "always in charge." The word "loving" is never included. When the list is complete, Dr. Hill draws a box around it, then asks the students to name words that men and boys are likely to hear when they step outside the Man Box. These words, too, are always the same: "bitch," "pussy," "fag." "We're boxed in here," Dr. Hill says. He encourages the group to think about wider options for how to be masculine, granting permission to "get out of the box."

The group then explores what this language reveals about power and dominance, and group members consider how much they themselves are afraid of being disrespected or attacked by other men. Finally, the discussion enlarges to an understanding of the hierarchy of gender. When sex is seen as conquest, the exercise concludes, sexual violence becomes an expression of the norm, not a deviation from it. According to Dr. Hill, this activity generates a lot of emotional engagement, as young men begin to see that changing patriarchal culture might benefit them as well as women. After completing this training, these students, working in pairs, can lead educational programs on masculinity and consent for fraternities, athletic teams, and other campus groups. They meet regularly with Dr. Hill for continued education and support.

Dr. Hill reports that he has recently trained a whole cohort of athletes and that many more fraternity members are coming to him, wanting to figure out how to hold members accountable for bad behavior. Some have even come to him privately to own up to having "caused harm" (the preferred language in MARS programs). "Folks are really interested in this," he says. "They don't think about it or realize they need it until you provide that heightened awareness." By now, he says, research on the effectiveness of peer education is well established, and he reports receiving many requests from other campuses that want to start similar peer education programs.[11]

On many campuses, sexual assault prevention efforts also include what is called bystander intervention, an effort to engage students not only as potential victims or perpetrators but also as members of the moral community with both the power and the responsibility to change the social norms of rape culture and to stop assaults before they happen. Like the MARS trainings, bystander intervention trainings understand sexual assault as a public health problem that requires a change in the entire social and cultural ecosystem.

Trainings focus first of all on helping students to identify high-risk situations and then on developing both the courage and the practical skills to intervene safely. Students discuss the main barrier to intervention: the fear of social ostracism for trying to change cultural norms. Then they practice action strategies for hypothetical common scenarios, like figuring out how to help a very intoxicated woman get home safely from a party where men are hitting on her, or speaking up directly when someone is bragging about coercing a woman into sex. Since 2013, when Congress mandated that educational institutions receiving federal funding include bystander intervention training as part of sexual assault prevention, these programs have proliferated. Some recent studies report encouraging outcome data suggesting that these programs are effective in changing both students' rape-supportive attitudes and their willingness to do something about potentially dangerous situations.[12]

One particularly promising study found that bystander intervention could actually reduce the incidence of violence on campus as well. This study compared a large state university (University of Kentucky) that had instituted bystander intervention training with two other public universities that had not. The training program was based on a "diffusion model" of peer education, the idea that changing attitudes and behavior among "peer opinion leaders" will have wide influence throughout the student body, so that it is not necessary to train everyone. While the training was open to all students, the program directors made a particular effort to recruit fraternity and sorority leaders, athletes involved in varsity sports, leaders of the student council and other organized activities, and those earning academic honors. A little over 15 percent of the student body participated in an intensive four- to six-hour training carried out in small groups. Apparently, this was enough to make a real difference. The researchers found that after several cohorts had been trained at the University of Kentucky, student reports of both perpetration and victimization on campus-wide anonymous surveys were significantly lower there than on the two campuses where no students had been trained.[13]

Thus, the first leg of the preventive tripod, the educational component, looks to be reasonably well developed and sturdy. By 2015, a survey of over eight hundred institutions of higher education, conducted by the American Association of Universities (AAU), reported that 61 percent had sexual assault prevention programs in place, including 92 percent of four-year public,

77 percent of historically Black, and 75 percent of four-year private nonprofit colleges and universities.[14]

The Tripod: Leg Two

The second leg of the tripod, effective response to survivors, is still a work in progress. The same AAU survey from 2015 found that in the previous decade, most institutions of higher education had expanded their response capabilities. Once again, public four-year institutions led the way: 100 percent had an official Title IX coordinator on staff, 99 percent offered some on-campus counseling for victims of sexual assault, and 83 percent had on-campus victim advocates. Private nonprofit four-year colleges were not far behind. In theory, at least, these campuses offered survivors a suitable range of options, from filing a formal complaint with the Title IX office to seeking confidential support from counselors or advocates. The question remains how often students avail themselves of these options and what happens when they do.

It seems clear that though many survivors seek help in a crisis, most do not wish to file a formal complaint that would result in disciplining the perpetrator. Their immediate wishes focus more on what *they* need to feel safe on campus. They frequently ask for the equivalent of civil restraining orders, so that they do not have to run into the perpetrator daily in classes or dormitories. If someone has to drop a class or move to another dorm, they ask, why should it always be the victim? In the aftermath of assault, many survivors also seek postponement of academic requirements. If they have acute stress disorder, haven't slept in a week, and can barely concentrate on their studies, the thought of writing a paper or taking a final exam may be completely overwhelming.

Reasonable accommodations help survivors feel that they still belong and that they matter to the college community; without them, many will feel that the campus effectively belongs to the perpetrators and will eventually drop out, as Rivera did.[15] Unfortunately, in the past, survivors seeking help have often encountered institutional responses ranging from merely insensitive to frankly dismissive and shaming. After all, from the point of view of many college administrators, sexual assault victims are simply a headache. They could compromise the school's reputation or, worse, its football season. They could even be a legal liability. It is so much more convenient if these victims can simply be made to keep quiet or, failing that, to go away.

Many anecdotal accounts from student survivors document the kind of bureaucratic nightmare that can ensue when they seek help. In 2014, the *Harvard Crimson* published a letter from Anonymous, a sexual assault survivor, titled "Dear Harvard: You Win." In it, she detailed numerous fruitless meetings with various deans in which she sought to have the offending student transferred to another dorm so that she did not have to fear encountering him every day in the dining hall, the library, or the laundry room. She made clear that she was *not* seeking disciplinary action against him, only accommodations for herself, which admittedly might cause him some inconvenience. She was basically told that nothing could be done unless she filed a formal complaint, but then she was advised not to file a formal complaint because, really, nothing could be done. Instead, she was advised to "forgive [the] assailant and move on."

Anonymous concluded that the administrators were not bad people, but they had no idea how to deal with cases of sexual assault. She wrote, "I may have lost my battle, but I also hope that this story can initiate a serious discussion about the way we want to handle cases like mine as a community. Do we really want to let survivors advocate for themselves until they are so exhausted that they collapse into depression?" She concluded, "Dear Harvard: You might have won, but I still have a voice. And I plan on using it as much as I can to make things change."[16]

A few days after the article was published, President Drew Faust (Harvard's first-ever female president after more than three hundred years) announced the formation of a Task Force on the Prevention of Sexual Assault. A year later, the task force reported that Harvard did indeed have a problem. As on so many other campuses, incidence of sexual assault was high, reporting was low, and female students did not trust that college officials would take a report seriously or treat them fairly. In an open meeting when this interim report was released, President Faust acknowledged that the university's responses to the problem were "completely insufficient" and vowed to engage the entire campus in making the necessary reforms.[17]

I share this anecdote as a heartening example of the way that survivors who speak out can sometimes initiate change. We will return to the matter of the task force and its final report when we discuss the third and wobbliest leg of the tripod, the question of disciplinary action. First, however, let us return to Northwestern University for a model from a campus that does seem to have a well-developed support center for sexual assault survivors. Kyra Jones, the artist and community activist whom we met in Chapter 6, worked there for three years as assistant director of the Center for Awareness, Response, and Education (CARE), a service based in the student affairs department. She saw her work as part of her own survivor mission: "CARE helped me when I was a student," she says, "and it was good to be able to pay it forward."

The CARE program offers supportive counseling and advocacy services for survivors of sexual assault and harassment, with strong protections for confidentiality. No information about the student's case is shared with academic or disciplinary authorities unless the student wishes to make a formal Title IX complaint. The assurance of confidentiality is particularly important because many colleges and universities, in an effort to counteract past histories of institutional passivity (and protect themselves from liability), now make it mandatory for faculty and staff to report any student disclosures of sexual assault to the administration, or even to the police, with or without the student's knowledge or consent. This can be just as much a betrayal as the indifference and inaction described by Anonymous, because it offers the student no choice in the matter and leaves her powerless.[18]

Besides individual counseling, the CARE center offers well-structured survivor support groups, a very useful treatment modality to counteract the shame and isolation that afflict so many traumatized people. If a student wishes to make a formal report to the separate Title IX office, a CARE advocate can offer informal support during the investigation process. Very few students decide to go this route, however. Jones reports that in the three years she worked at CARE, she advised only one student who chose this path. Most students mainly want (and receive) help with academics, housing, and no-contact orders for their own protection and peace of mind. CARE can also help survivors connect with the Title IX office to request that they call in the "responsible" student for an "informal conversation," without a formal report. This, too, is confidential.

Having been a CARE peer counselor when she was a student at Northwestern, Jones became an adviser and trainer for thirty to forty student volunteers. Their rigorous curriculum was equivalent to a full-semester course, complete with outside speakers and a written exam. The students seemed to love the training, even though they didn't get any course credit for it. She clearly loved the students, whom she describes as intense, creative, and highly motivated.

Some of the educational activities led by the peer counselors include a play titled *The Student Body*, written and performed by students during freshman orientation. Following the performance, CARE staff members lead breakout groups to discuss issues of rape culture, consent, and bystander intervention. "This is real prevention work," says Jones, "not: 'don't drink at parties.'" A CARE mobile unit called "Find the G-Spot" drives around the campus, giving out safer-sex supplies like condoms and counseling students on sexual health. CARE also sponsors special events, often collaborating with student groups. In 2019, their invited speaker was Tarana Burke, founder of Me Too International. These prevention activities raise student consciousness about both the problem of sexual assault and how to seek help if needed. Jones reflects, "I've definitely seen a change in the campus culture since I was a student." This encouraging example indicates that preventive education and survivor-centered support services can indeed help to create a safer and more equitable campus community.

The Tripod: Leg Three

Now comes the hard part: enforcement. Attempts to discipline students who commit sexual assault, like all other attempts to hold perpetrators accountable, have been highly contentious, provoking strong backlash and lots and lots of lawsuits.

At Harvard, for example, the task force convened in 2014 to address the problem of sexual assault on campus submitted its final report in 2016. Much to my surprise, it did actually tackle the hard questions. It recognized the dangers of having student social life centered in "male-dominated spaces" and singled out the all-male "final clubs"—Harvard's equivalent of fraternities, whose exclusiveness and prestige gave them the reputation for having the best parties—as particularly high-frequency environments for target rape. (I am told that they are called final clubs because membership represents the final step of admission into the elite of the elite. JFK was a member of the Spee Club, FDR was a member of the Fly, and Teddy Roosevelt was a member of the most final of all, the Porcellian.) The dean of the college, Rakesh Khurana, who advocated sanctioning the clubs for institutionalized sex discrimination, wrote, "The most entrenched of these spaces send an unambiguous message that they are the exclusive preserves of men. In their recruitment practices and through their extensive resources and access to networks of power, these organizations propagate exclusionary values."[19]

The final clubs, located in elegant buildings nested within the campus, are independent organizations, with no official Harvard oversight. Prohibiting students from joining them was never considered, since that would infringe on the students' rights of free association. Instead, the college gave all single-sex student clubs a choice: either to become co-ed or to be subject to sanctions that would bar club members from holding leadership positions in Harvard student groups and on athletic teams and make them ineligible for recommendations for certain prestigious fellowships. All the campus women's groups decided to integrate, but, with few exceptions, the all-male clubs dug in their heels and refused to admit women. Instead, they sued Harvard in state and federal courts for—what else—sex discrimination under Title IX.

Both as an effort to promote change in the campus culture and as a more specific effort to discipline the final clubs, Harvard's initiative was unsuccessful. In 2019, a large-scale anonymous student survey of thirty-three schools and 180,000 students conducted by the American Association of Universities found that the rates of sexual assault at Harvard were unchanged from four years earlier and that most students still did not report incidents of sexual misconduct.[20] In 2020, after noting that recent Supreme Court decisions made it unlikely that Harvard would prevail in court against the final clubs, the college quietly rescinded its sanctions policy.[21] At the present writing, no other disciplinary initiative has been undertaken.

Harvard was not alone in its inability to develop clear and effective disciplinary policies for sexual assault. Nationally, the main disciplinary question of the moment seems to be whether educational institutions should be required to follow the same rules and procedures in their Title IX investigations as criminal courts when dealing with students accused of sexual assault. To me, it seems obvious that the answer is no. The terrible track record of criminal courts in sexual assault cases would be reason enough to look for something better. But there are additional reasons. The majority of sexual assault survivors do not necessarily want harsh sanctions, and they avoid seeking official disciplinary action both for their own sake and for the sake of the offenders. They don't want to get these young men into serious trouble, but they do want accountability in some form, and educational institutions are in a unique position to develop new and better ways of holding offenders accountable.

Colleges and universities are voluntary communities. Higher education is a privilege, not a right. Schools have their own specific conduct rules for inclusion. Plagiarism, for example, is forbidden. When the rules are violated, the most serious disciplinary consequence for students is expulsion; for faculty it would be termination of a job. No one's liberty is at stake, as it is in criminal courts. Those accused of sexual misconduct are entitled to reasonable due process protections, as in civil law, but they do not have the same legal rights as criminal defendants; nor should they. Legal scholar and activist Alexandra Brodsky argues that sexual assault and harassment should be understood basically as civil rights violations and treated similarly to harassment on the basis of race, gender orientation, or disability. Since both the complainant and the respondent have an equal stake in being able to pursue their education at the institution, they should be afforded equal due process rights in disciplinary proceedings.[22]

Nevertheless, as in other situations where impunity is threatened, advocates for the perpetrators mobilized politically to expand the rights of the accused under what I have named the narrative of the Fine Young Man. This is another version of the familiar tactic of DARVO (Deny, Attack, Reverse Victim and Offender): What happened was sex, not rape. She asked for it. She is a slut. She is crazy. Or maybe she's just out for revenge because he dropped her, and everyone knows that hell hath no fury, and so forth. The true victim is the Fine Young Man, whose life is about to be ruined by this "witch hunt." Of course, in this instance the witches are supposedly doing the hunting, which would be a historic first, but never mind. Some judges seem to find this argument persuasive. For instance, a New Jersey Superior Court judge recently denied a prosecutor's motion to charge as an adult a sixteen-year-old boy who filmed himself on his phone raping an intoxicated girl at a party, because he came from a "good family" and was "a candidate for a good college." (An appeals court later rebuked him.)[23]

Under the Donald Trump administration, the US Department of Education (DOE) embraced this narrative. Secretary of Education Betsy de Vos, appearing with distraught mothers of Fine Young Men who had been disciplined for sexual assault, promulgated new rules that made it *more* difficult for schools to hold students accountable under Title IX. The main effect of the rule changes was to narrow the definitions of what counted as sexual misconduct, requiring that students be subjected to harassment that was "severe, pervasive, and objectively offensive" before a school had an obligation to take action. The new rules also added numerous protections for the accused, including the right to confront and cross-examine their accusers in person. The new regulations also favored a higher evidentiary standard for sexual assault cases (clear and convincing evidence) rather than the balanced standard (preponderance of evidence) that prevails in civil law.

Before finalizing these new rules, the DOE was required to allow public comment on the proposed regulations. They received over one hundred thousand comments from individuals and organizations, an unusually large number, indicating how contentious this issue had become. I myself contributed a comment letter that was circulated by the National Women's Law Center and signed within seventy-two hours by over nine hundred colleagues in the mental health professions. Most of the letter writers opposed the new regulations. As the American Association of Universities wrote in its comment letter, requiring schools to create adversarial "quasi-courts" would not create a fairer process for seeking the truth and would make it harder for schools to protect students from sexual assault and harassment.

It seemed that this was actually the desired result. The DOE went ahead and finalized the new rules anyway in 2020. The Joe Biden administration is now seeking to reverse them. In response to litigation from a coalition of women's advocacy groups challenging these new regulations, a federal court judge has already vacated one of the most oppressive rules, which excluded any evidence supplied by anyone who refused to submit to live cross-examination (including the respondent). In striking down this provision, Judge William Young wrote that this rule would severely hamper Title IX investigations, turning them into "a remarkably hollow gesture."[24]

It appears, however, that the new restrictive rules have already had their intended effect, helping to make Title IX disciplinary actions almost as rare as criminal convictions for sexual assault. Rowan Frost, who directs the Sexual Health, Advocacy and Relationship Education program at Reed College, estimates that if the school has one hundred sexual assaults per year, twenty to forty will be reported, three to five will go through a disciplinary hearing, and one to two students will be disciplined.[25] Paradoxically, however, while narrowing the official definition of what "counts" as sexual assault or harassment may have discouraged official Title IX investigations, it has opened the door for more informal and creative ways of responding to sexual misconduct that doesn't fit within the narrowed guidelines.

The Restorative Justice Alternative

Educators on many campuses are considering whether restorative justice (RJ) concepts can be adapted to find truly educational ways of holding young offenders accountable. They reason that harsh punishments like expulsion will only harden these young men in their defensiveness and may increase the risk that they will reoffend somewhere else, whereas keeping young offenders within the educational community with clear consequences for their behavior may offer them the best path to moral development. (RJ may be more appropriate for sexual assaults between acquaintances, which are often single incidents, than for other forms of gender-based violence that occur in the context of an ongoing relationship of coercive control.) Advocates for RJ argue that this form of accountability holds the promise of repairing the harms not only to the victim but also to the campus community.

Meg Bossong, Title IX coordinator at Williams College, describes an "alternative resolution" option for students who report sexual assault, stalking, or harassment. They are given support in order to develop an impact statement that will be read aloud to the respondent. The reading can take place either in a healing circle or, more commonly, via a kind of "shuttle diplomacy," where the RJ facilitator speaks to the respondent on behalf of the reporter. (Most reporters do *not* want to have a face-to-face encounter, she finds, so the "shuttle" option is appealing to them.) The disciplinary outcome for the respondent is usually assignment to an educational program on gender, sexual assault, and consent in sexual relations, with completion of the program as a requirement for graduation. He is also assigned the difficult "emotional labor" of coming up with a plan for making amends that is acceptable to the reporter. This may take several tries, as the respondent incorporates feedback from the reporter. The process requires him to think about the impact of his behavior on another person and to imagine what he can do to atone for it. In other words, the program requires him to develop his capacity for empathy.

The process is finalized with a written agreement, in which the respondent acknowledges responsibility to repair the harm that was done. Interestingly, the respondent is *not* required to acknowledge responsibility for actually *causing* the harm, thus finessing an admission that might leave him open to criminal prosecution. This, of course, makes the RJ option more appealing to him. The survivors who participate seem to understand that this is a legal technicality and that if the RJ process is unsatisfactory, the option of a criminal complaint is still available.

Bossong is clear about the limitations of this approach. First of all, she asserts that RJ is not for everyone. She rules out respondents who persist in denial or show signs of sociopathy, as well as repeat offenders and those who have used weapons. Second, she thinks it unrealistic to expect that the circle process by itself will be sufficient to prevent similar assaults from happening again (a point on which Kyra Jones would surely agree). Ideally, she says, the school should take on the responsibility for careful follow-up with the respondent, monitoring his conduct to make sure that he fulfills the terms of his reparations agreement throughout his time at the school.[26]

Bossong is also clear on the point that the RJ alternative resolution is not the same as mediation, with which it is often confused. This distinction is critically important, for both conceptual and practical reasons. In mediation, both parties to the conflict are presumed to bear some responsibility for the problem, and the facilitator takes a neutral stance between them. In restorative justice, by contrast, the facilitator recognizes that there is a reporter and a respondent, a harm-doer and a person who has been harmed. The stance of the facilitator is not neutral; rather the facilitator represents the moral community in vindicating the person who has been harmed and holding the harm-doer responsible. The challenge for the RJ facilitator is to show respect and empathy for both parties while at the same time representing community disapproval of the harm-doer's actions and insisting on the need for repair.

The practical reasons for making a clear distinction between RJ and mediation have to do with the Department of Education's regulations for resolution of Title IX complaints. Until recently, the DOE's guidelines specifically prohibited mediation for sexual assault incidents. The point of these guidelines was to prevent the all-too-common practice of holding the victim at least as responsible as the perpetrator (What did she expect, going out dressed like that?). But many college administrators were confused about the difference between RJ and mediation, and therefore they were reluctant to explore RJ as a potential alternative to formal Title IX disciplinary action. More recently, in line with other efforts to minimize discipline for offenders, the DOE has explicitly given permission for informal resolution of sexual assault complaints. This may facilitate wider implementation and more systematic study of the effectiveness of RJ in the future.

Professor David Karp, author of *The Little Book of Restorative Justice for Colleges and Universities*,[27] has long been a strong advocate for RJ as the best hope for responding to complaints in a way that promotes serious change in rape culture. He points out, quite correctly, that not all sexual assaults are target rapes. Many assaults are not premeditated; the young men who commit them are ignorant about issues of gender and power, sexually inexperienced, and morally immature. Add copious amounts of alcohol, and you have a perfect recipe for hookups gone wrong. Karp argues that these young people are not hardened offenders and can be educated to do better.

As a representative illustration, Karp presents the hypothetical case of "Kevin" and "Amy," students who meet at a campus party. Seeing that Amy is quite intoxicated, Kevin walks her to her room. Amy consents to sex—in fact, she makes the first move—but once they are in bed, complications arise. Amy rushes to the bathroom, apparently to throw up, and when she comes back to bed, she becomes quite unresponsive. Kevin wonders whether she has passed out. Nevertheless, he proceeds to have intercourse with her. The next day, she has no recall of what happened. When Kevin thanks her for the "wild night," she is furious with him for taking advantage of her when she was drunk, and she files a complaint with the school. Here is a case that falls into what is commonly considered a "gray area." Might not Kevin be forgiven for thinking this was just a *misunderstanding*? Surely, this wouldn't "count" as sexual assault, would it? After all, she did say yes, and how could he be expected to judge whether she was too intoxicated to consent?

Actually, it's not that difficult a call. Look at it this way, Kevin: Would you think it was a good idea for Amy to drive a car in the state she was in when you had sex with her? And more to the point, would you think it was a good idea to get in the car with her and go along for the ride? Having intercourse with someone who is too intoxicated to consent actually does "count." In terms of the law, in many states it is indeed a criminal offense, as well as a violation of the school's conduct code.

But that in some ways is beside the point. No one in this scenario wants to get Kevin in trouble with the law. Not Amy (usually), not the school, and of course not Kevin. Adolescents do many stupid things, including getting into cars and driving drunk. The point of moral education is to help develop their immature frontal lobes, which are the biological foundation for capacities like insight, judgment, understanding another person's perspective, and empathizing with another person's feelings. What Amy wants from Kevin is an acknowledgment of harm and an assurance that he has learned his lesson. What she needs from the school is moral support and an institutional structure that can help Kevin understand that what he did was wrong and require him to make amends.

Karp points out that in this case, harsh disciplinary action is likely to make Kevin feel he has been treated unfairly, to increase his defensive rationalizations for his behavior, and to polarize the student friendship networks, with one group calling Kevin a rapist and the other calling Amy a liar. On the other hand, he argues, a restorative justice approach that focuses on repairing the harm has the potential to provide accountability "in a way that leverages social support and leads to healing for individuals and a safer campus climate for living and learning."[28]

Hopefully this alternative process would engage Kevin to reflect on his own motivations and entitlements. He might be invited to reconsider the belief that when a man is sexually excited, he can't be expected to stop, even if his partner is unconscious. He might also talk about the social pressure he feels to get laid in order to have bragging rights among his male friends. He might gain the courage to apologize. Amy might feel heard and vindicated, and she might gain trust that Kevin will not do this again. Both students might feel valued and respected; neither would feel driven out of the campus community.

Based on prototypes of this kind, Karp proposes that RJ practices like healing circles be implemented widely on college campuses as a method of secondary prevention, leaving harsher sanctions only for repeated offenses and cases of sexual assault where there is clear evidence of premeditation. In a recent article, along with colleagues from other campuses, he offers guidelines for developing RJ programs, outlining procedures for ensuring that participation is truly voluntary for both parties, reviewing the legal boundaries of confidentiality, and offering templates for the reparation agreements that the students will sign.[29]

At present, we have no large studies with outcome data on the comparative effectiveness of RJ alternative disciplinary programs for sexual assault on college campuses. Such programs are still too early in their development. The potential is there, however, for innovative adaptations, well-designed outcome studies, and wider dissemination of successful programs. Such programs offer a model for how the weakest leg of the preventive tripod, effective discipline, could become stronger and fairer to all concerned. Of course, even if campus RJ programs are shown to be effective, adapting them to many other institutions and scaling them up to the wider society will still be an enormous challenge. Think of these programs, then, as the first stage in basic social science research on novel methods of implementing cultural change.

In summary: institutions of higher education seem like ideal laboratories in which to imagine new ways of addressing the endemic social problem of sexual assault, with both a social justice mission of promoting gender equity and a public health mission of violence prevention. In the difficult work of challenging deeply entrenched social customs that ritualize the rules of tyranny, college campuses can help to create new social customs of mutuality and develop institutional practices that inspire trust. And trust, in turn, is the foundation of a just and democratic moral community.

CONCLUSION:
THE LONGEST REVOLUTION

As for me, my journey has brought me to the point of believing unequivocally . . . that women's lives have value, that ending gender-based violence is the only way to achieve true equality . . . [and] that we can end gender violence.

—Anita Hill, *Believing*[1]

More than fifty years ago, I read a little pamphlet titled "Women: The Longest Revolution," written by British author and psychologist Juliet Mitchell. In it, she clarified to her "brothers" on the left why women's liberation was so much more complicated than simply empowering the working class. Whereas workers are oppressed in the domain of production, she explained, women are oppressed in four domains: production, reproduction, sex, and child rearing. Progress in one domain, she added, could be undermined by reaction in another. As an example, she cited the Soviet Union, where women's public advancement in the workplace was undermined by reactionary policies in so-called private matters of reproduction and sex. The longest revolution, to succeed, required women's empowerment in all four domains.[2]

How have we progressed in half a century of this longest revolution? Worldwide, we have at least the token recognition that women's rights are human rights, thanks to the Convention on the Elimination of All Forms of Discrimination Against Women, passed by the United Nations General Assembly in 1979 and ratified by ninety-nine countries, with the notable exceptions of Saudi Arabia and the United States. Article I states that discrimination means "any distinction, exclusion or restriction made on the basis of sex which has the effect or purpose of impairing or nullifying the recognition, enjoyment or exercise by women, irrespective of their marital status, on a basis of equality of men and women, of human rights and fundamental freedoms in the political, economic, social, cultural, civil or any other field." The convention also sets up a mechanism for signatory states to report on their progress every four years.[3]

In the public domain, the convention focuses on the right to vote and to hold office in government, as well as to equal education and to participation in the public labor force. It also covers the private domains of reproduction and child care, stating that reproductive choice is a civil right for women and that both sexes have equal responsibilities for child rearing. Only the domain of sex is not mentioned; the United Nations is still reserved on the matter of female pleasure. But as we learned in Chapter 3, it has now recognized sexual violence as a worldwide scourge.

In 1994, the United Nations created the position of special rapporteur on violence against women to survey progress in this domain. Fifteen years later, in 2009, Special Rapporteur Yakin Erturk reported, "The unfortunate fact remains that, for the most part, violence against women continues to be perpetrated with impunity, access to justice is ridden with obstacles, and accountability remains elusive within the domestic realm."[4] In a progress report at the twenty-five-year mark, in 2019, Special Rapporteur Dubravka Simonovic wrote, "At present, at the international normative level, the right of women to be free from violence is recognized as an international human rights standard, but in practice, gender-based violence against women and girls continues to be tolerated and [is] normalized in many societies."[5] In other words, more countries now pay lip service to the ideas of women's rights, but moving beyond this point requires cultural changes at the deepest level.

What about progress in the United States? At the time of the Second Wave of the feminist movement, women at demonstrations often wore buttons with the figure "59¢." That stood for the average pay for women in the workforce compared to every dollar for men. By 1990, it had risen all the way to sixty-four cents. Now, according to the US Department of Labor, white, non-Hispanic women earn on average 79 percent of what white, non-Hispanic men earn. Black women earn 63 percent, and Hispanic women earn 55 percent.[6] That would be one metric of progress. At this rate, white women might achieve parity by 2070 or thereabouts, and Black women, fifty years later.

In many public domains of production—business, academia, the professions, government, and the military—women's representation has grown, in many cases, from token representation or none at all toward an intermediate stage in the range of 20 to 30 percent, but not to full integration. The higher one goes in the pyramid of power and wealth, the lower the percentage of women. And at many of the lowest-paid levels of the workforce, one still finds a majority of women, especially women of color.

I have a theory that as women move past the level of token representation in many parts of the public domain, speaking out about violence and exploitation begins, and so does what I have come to call housecleaning, an incipient form of justice that at the very least tries to expose and denounce the most notorious predators and remove them from their positions of power. It's dirty work, but someone has to do it. That was certainly true in my own profession. In the early 1980s, the proportion of women in psychiatry crossed the 15 percent threshold. Not coincidentally, I believe, the Committee on Women of the American Psychiatric Association (APA) found its voice, moving from what was essentially a support group for token women to an activist group that demanded accountability from the male-dominated leadership. We had all seen cases of sexual exploitation of patients by prominent psychiatrists, and we decided the profession needed cleaning up.

Shirley Chisholm, the first Black woman elected to Congress, was known to say, "If they don't give you a seat at the table, bring a folding chair." Following this mantra, in 1982, I and other members of our committee approached the board of directors of the APA, uninvited. We asked for official approval to conduct a national survey of psychiatrists' sexual involvement with patients. The board declined our proposal; the only person who seemed to recognize the seriousness of the problem was the legal counsel, and that was because patients had begun to file malpractice lawsuits that were costing the organization some serious money.

Not taking no for an answer, my colleagues Nanette Gartrell and Silvia Olarte and I decided to do the survey ourselves, without the auspices of any professional organization, and we raised the funds to do it. Promised anonymity, over fourteen hundred psychiatrists from all around the country responded to our random sample survey. We found that about 7 percent of male and 3 percent of female psychiatrists acknowledged sexual relationships with one or more patients, with 95 percent of the cases involving male psychiatrists. The *American Journal of Psychiatry's* editor, John Nemiah, bravely published our report in 1986, after sending it out to seven reviewers (the average number is two or three), all of whom said that, try as they might, they couldn't find anything wrong with our methodology.[7] This is a very Second Wave sort of story. We like to think that as a result of our troublemaking, a few alpha males in our profession quietly surrendered their medical licenses.

Here are a few additional statistics that bear out my housecleaning hypothesis, all drawn from sectors of our society where fifty years ago women were either entirely absent or a token presence. In the US military, women now constitute 21 percent of the "airmen" in the air force, 20 percent of navy sailors, and 15 percent of army soldiers.[8] As these thresholds have been crossed, housecleaning has taken the form of more and more reports of what is now called military sexual trauma. In the US Congress, where women now constitute 24 percent of the Senate and 27 percent of the House of Representatives, there has been a lot of housecleaning to do. It has taken the form of changing the laws and procedures of military justice that have resulted in impunity for perpetrators of sexual harassment and violence in the armed services. Women from both parties took the lead in this initiative, which finally prevailed in 2021 after years of resistance from the military brass. And in the film industry, where women in 2016 constituted 17 percent of all directors, writers, producers, executive producers, and cinematographers in the top 250 films, housecleaning has taken the form of public exposure of many prominent serial predators at the top levels of Hollywood and other sectors of the media and worldwide amplification of the movement, begun by Black women, called #MeToo.

In a *New York Times* op-ed, Catharine MacKinnon observed that #MeToo had accomplished something that legal reforms alone could not. "Revulsion against harassing behavior," she wrote, "could change workplaces and schools. It could restrain repeat predators as well as the occasional and casual exploiters that so far the law has not. Shunning perpetrators as sex bigots who take advantage of the vulnerabilities of inequality could transform society. It could change rape culture."[9] One might consider these recent developments a combination of progress in the intersecting domains of production and sex and the beginnings of a new form of justice that can put an end to impunity.

In the domain of reproduction, feminists gained national legal recognition of the rights to contraception and abortion early in the Second Wave and have been on the defensive ever since, with a backlash that has gained more and more political power over the years. Now, as I write, although a majority of the public supports abortion rights, the authoritarian majority on the Supreme Court (including, of course, the two justices who notoriously symbolize impunity and injustice for survivors of sexual violence) has just voided this legal precedent that has prevailed nationally for half a century. Their decision will allow many states to criminalize abortion once again. This follows an international pattern in which retrograde laws controlling reproduction are promoted by minority right-wing populist movements that ally with religious groups to degrade democracy.[10]

In the domain of child care, my impression is that virtually no progress has been made in fifty years. The work of caretaking is still women's work, it is still privatized, and it is still devalued. How many more lifetimes will it take to end the subordination of women?

The Survivors' Agenda

I have argued that survivors of gender-based violence can take the lead on envisioning justice for women because they have seen up close the injustice of a patriarchal order and understand the profound cultural and political changes that are needed for the longest revolution. One recent development affirms this idea. In 2017, the leaders of four major grassroots organizations, women of color who have publicly identified themselves as survivors of sexual violence, came together as a collective to develop what they call the Survivors' Agenda. They conducted numerous focus groups as well as an online survey to consult with survivors about their wishes. In July 2020, Tarana Burke, founder and executive director of Me Too International, and Monica Ramirez, founder and president of Justice for Migrant Women, wrote, "The fight to end racism and the fight to end sexual violence are inextricably linked. The Survivors' Agenda will write a new chapter in this story of liberation."[11] It stands to reason that women of color, living at the intersection of two profoundly embedded systems of oppression, could be uniquely positioned to bring together the twin movements for Black lives and women's lives that for so long have been divided from one another.

Convening a three-day virtual summit meeting in September 2020, Ramirez declared, "It is time for survivors to come together to create the vision of a world without violence." Justice, in this radical vision, means nothing less than an end to patriarchal and racist systems of dominance and subordination, revealing the violence at their heart and repairing their profound harms. With twelve thousand people in attendance, keynote speaker Anita Hill said, "In my experience, there has never been anything like this. I have been waiting for this for a long time."

Countless women have been waiting for this moment for a long time. It has been inspiring in my old age to witness a radical feminist awakening much like the Second Wave of my youth, only stronger, broader, deeper. In speaking the words "me too," survivors are recognizing that they are not alone, they have nothing to be ashamed of, and theirs is not a private misfortune. They are naming the hidden violence that maintains patriarchal systems and demanding that bystanders in the moral community stand up to put an end to it.

The thirty-page Survivors' Agenda published in 2020 is a blueprint for the future of the longest revolution. The agenda addresses all the domains of women's oppression. Regarding production, it calls for the rights of the most vulnerable: domestic workers, tipped workers, undocumented workers. Regarding child rearing, the Survivors' Agenda calls for public investment in widely accessible and affordable day care and livable wages for those who provide care. Regarding reproduction, it calls for universal health insurance and unfettered access to contraception and abortion. Anticipating the Supreme Court ruling, in a June 2022 teach-in linking survivors' justice and reproductive justice, Tarana Burke reminded her audience that "movements build on the hope—look for the strategy. You don't sit in your setback, you strategize about how you will move forward."

With regard to sex, once again the Survivors' Agenda's focus is on the most vulnerable women, those sold in prostitution, who are disproportionately women of color. Because the police as well as pimps and johns prey upon those who are euphemistically called sex workers, the Survivors' Agenda calls for decriminalization of consensual exchanges of sex for money. In my mind, the key word in the Survivors' Agenda position is "consensual." As we have seen in Chapter 7, it is debatable how many girls and women freely consent to prostitution, since they are mostly recruited from situations of racial subordination, desperate poverty, childhood abuse, and homelessness. Moreover, considering that on average recruitment into prostitution worldwide takes place in early to mid-adolescence, most recruits are not in a legal position to give consent.[12] Even most libertarians do not advocate decriminalizing child abuse (though some "sex-positive" writers do).

I would argue, therefore, that the Nordic model is quite compatible with the Survivors' Agenda. I would also argue that it is more compatible with the agenda of healing justice, for the Swedish law provides robust access to health and mental health care, housing, and vocational and educational services for people who have been prostituted, as well as education for both the police and the public about the harms of the sex industry.[13] In this regard, the law might be considered analogous to the "tripod" model of prevention and public health discussed in Chapter 9.

The radical vision of justice that has emerged from the Survivors' Agenda is centered on safety and healing for survivors rather than punishment of offenders. It struggles honestly with the most difficult question: how to put a stop to abusive behavior, all the while respecting the humanity of both those who have done harm and those who have been harmed. Its vision of justice is basically congruent with the vision that emerges from my own interviews with survivors. It recognizes the need for the existing structures of community safety, at least at present. It does not call for abolition of police, courts, or even prisons.

The Survivors' Agenda does call for a fundamental "reimagining [of] how communities address safety" and for creation of alternatives to the "criminal legal system," centered on the healing of survivors rather than punishment of offenders. It calls for imagining new ways to hold perpetrators to account without caging or exiling them or denying their humanity, although it recognizes that scalable models of these new forms of accountability do not yet exist. It calls for a renewed moral community, where bystanders forgo the easy path of complicity with those who dominate to stand unequivocally with those who have been subordinated. Finally, it calls for determined community investment in public health and education to transform the culture

that glorifies white male supremacy and to prevent sexual
lence by addressing its "root causes."

This is the radical survivors' vision of justice. It challenges
of us to begin dismantling our most deeply embedded stru
tures of oppression and to create new structures where every
one is respected, everyone is included, and everyone has a voice.
When a person has been a victim of violence, survivors' justice
challenges us all to think first of all about centering justice on
that person in order to make reparations for the harm and to
provide what is needed for healing. Survivors need truth and
repair—acknowledgment, vindication, apology, and amends—
from their moral communities. When the community comes
through with these reparations, the damaged relationship between the community and the survivor is healed, trust is restored, and a better kind of justice is done.

The root causes of violence are the rules of tyranny. Prevention requires us to learn and practice the rules of mutuality,
rules that form the basis of trust and justice in a democratic society. These are the rules that benefit everyone, and we all would
be fortunate to live by them.

vio-

all

ACKNOWLEDGMENTS

When my father, Naphtali Lewis, spoke at his eightieth birthday celebration, he proposed that the secrets of longevity were four: genes, geography, luck, and love. Now, as I have reached that age myself, I have begun to realize how much one's path in life depends on the accidents of one's time and place and what a debt is owed to those who came before. So I begin by acknowledging my gratitude to my family of origin, for all the love, support, gifts, and privileges that made it possible for me to pursue my own path.

Over a century ago, during that lost time when the United States welcomed immigrants fleeing persecution, my grandparents left their homes in the Pale of Settlement in eastern Europe and joined the "huddled masses" who were greeted by Lady Liberty in New York Harbor and were given new American names at Ellis Island. In New York City they found a place where the immigrant's American dream could be realized and where their courage and hard work were rewarded with opportunity for the next generation.

I owe a particular debt to my maternal grandfather, whom I never knew and for whom I am named. Yehuda Bloch (renamed John Block), who arrived alone in 1887 at age seventeen, worked as a salesman while he learned English and saved money to go to medical school. Eventually, he became a general practitioner on the Lower East Side. He married Rose Boorstein, who had come to New York with her large family. As the oldest girl, Rose had had to leave school after sixth grade to help care for her five younger siblings, and throughout her life she felt inferior because she was uneducated. Together, my grandparents vowed that their children, girls as well as boys, would have a college education. And indeed, their daughter, Helen, thrived in the academic world, graduating from Barnard College and then gaining a doctorate in psychology from Columbia. I have wondered sometimes whether, if she had been born a generation later, she would have followed in her father's footsteps and become a physician. When I told her, as an adolescent, that I wanted to become a psychologist like her, she told me to go to medical school instead. "You'll have more power that way," she said, and of course she was right. And of course, though I didn't realize it then, she wanted me to follow the path of her adored father, who died before I was born.[1]

My paternal grandparents, Rebecca Leff and Isser (renamed "Ike") Lifschitz, found work in the factories of New York, where they saved money to bring their younger siblings over from Poland. I remember little about them, because they died while I was still young, but I do remember that Grandpa Lifschitz was a devoted member of his temple and also of the International Ladies' Garment Workers' Union. I still have as a keepsake a little plaster bust of Franklin D. Roosevelt, which was one of the only ornaments in their bare Bronx apartment. They, too, aspired to better things for their children, and both their sons became college professors. Naphtali, who Americanized his last name to Lewis, thrived in New York's famed public education system, including at City College, which was then entirely tuition-free. Having discovered early his gift for languages, he received his doctorate in classics at the Sorbonne and then returned to New York, where he spent his life teaching in the city's public university system. At one point he was offered a job at a prestigious private college, but he turned it down, explaining that he would rather teach students like himself who came from the working classes.

With two such parents as Naphtali and Helen, I was raised in the heady post–World War II cultural environment of New York's left-wing intelligentsia, a precious inheritance that at the time I took entirely for granted. I still remember my naïve astonishment the first time I entered a friend's home that was *not* filled with books. From my father I learned most of what I know about the beauty and precision of language. From my mother I learned the basics of psychology and scientific inquiry. From both I learned all I needed to know about courage and integrity, who had it and who did not, when they and many of their friends and colleagues faced persecution during the years of the McCarthy inquisition. I also learned an indelible lesson about the importance of living in a constitutional democracy with a Bill of Rights and the rule of law, institutions that offered some protection against the power of demagogues.

Both parents were ambitious for me and encouraged me in my own migration, from my home city to the very different world that I found at Harvard University. Despite the initial culture shock (this was in the days when Harvard still had quotas on

Jews), I found mentors and lifelong friends there, both at Radcliffe College and at Harvard Medical School (HMS). Eventually, much to my surprise, I joined the clinical faculty of the medical school, and within the university's capacious teaching hospitals, I found a place to build a professional community. So I owe a profound debt of gratitude as well to this institution that fostered me and gave me an intellectual home.

That home, for most of the past forty years, has been the Victims of Violence (VoV) Program in the Department of Psychiatry at Cambridge Health Alliance, one of the HMS teaching hospitals. I am filled with gratitude for the generosity and dedication of my colleagues there. I always tell people who want to work in the trauma field never to work alone. If you are going to witness the worst of what human beings are capable of, you will need to surround yourself with people who exemplify the best. Otherwise you will eventually give in to despair. My sisters and brothers at VoV have been a constant source of inspiration, not only in the clinic, but also onstage (mounting a production of V-Day) and on the water (rowing for Cambridge Hospital in dragon boat races). We have cried and laughed together and celebrated one another's marriages and the births of our children and now, for some of us elders, grandchildren. Many have become lifelong friends.

I am also indebted to a number of friends, colleagues, and family members who encouraged me and gave me critical feedback in the process of writing this book. Robert Jay Lifton and Frank Putnam gave me thoughtful advice early on. Diane Rosenfeld organized a daylong workshop with me to brainstorm about the idea of the college campus as a laboratory for new visions of justice. Orli and Reuven Avi-Yonah, Melissa Farley, David Konstan, Karen Messing, and Pratyusha Tummala-Narra read early drafts and gave me many useful suggestions. My dear friend Emily Schatzow, who has been my closest colleague for the past fifty years, was unfailing in her support, including offering criticism as needed. My brother, John Block Lewis, and my daughter, Emma Lewis Berndt, were always there for encouragement and brainstorming when I needed it most.

I had never worked with an agent before, but Elias Altman understood the book immediately and helped me immeasurably. Lara Heimert, my editor, was the consummate professional, all the while caring for a small child during a pandemic. To the extent that this book has a coherent, logical, and comprehensible argument, much of the credit belongs to her. The errors and defects, of course, are mine.

Most of all, of course, I am indebted to the thirty informants who shared their stories and their visions with me and to all my students and my patients, who over the years have taught me most of what I know.

NOTES

Introduction

1. J L Herman: *Trauma and Recovery: The Aftermath of Violence—from Domestic Abuse to Political Terror*. New York: Basic Books, 1992, 1997, 2015, 2022.

2. R J Lifton: *Death in Life: Survivors of Hiroshima*. Chapel Hill, NC: University of North Carolina Press, 1969, 1991.

3. United Nations: *The World's Women 2015: Trends and Statistics*. Department of Economic and Social Affairs, Statistics Division, 2015.

4. G Paley: "Two Ears, Three Lucks." *The Collected Stories*. New York: Farrar, Straus & Giroux, 1994, p. xi.

5. K Sarachild: "Consciousness-Raising: A Radical Weapon." In: *Feminist Revolution*. New York: Redstockings, 1975. As one of her first acts of radical feminism, Kathie renamed herself for her mother rather than her father.

6. D J Henderson: "Incest." In: A M Freedman, H I Kaplan & B J Sadock (Eds.): *Comprehensive Textbook of Psychiatry*, 2nd Edition. Baltimore: Williams & Wilkins, 1975, p. 1532.

7. J L Herman & L Hirschman: Father-daughter incest. *Signs: Journal of Women in Culture and Society* 1977; 2:735–756.

8. S Brownmiller: *Against Our Will: Men, Women, and Rape*. New York: Simon & Schuster, 1975. L Walker: *The Battered Woman*. New York: William Morrow, 1979. C MacKinnon: *Sexual Harassment of Working Women*. New Haven, CT: Yale University Press, 1979.

9. This and several other autobiographical passages first appeared in J L Herman: Helen Block Lewis: A memoir of three generations. *Psychoanalytic Psychology* 2013; 30:528–534.

10. K Crenshaw: "How R. Kelly Got Away with It," *New York Times*, October 3, 2021.

A Note About Methodology

1. J L Herman: Justice from the victim's perspective. *Violence Against Women* 2005; 11:571–602.

Chapter One: The Rules of Tyranny

1. T Snyder: *On Tyranny: Twenty Lessons from the Twentieth Century.* New York: Penguin Random House, 2017.

2. A D Biderman: Communist attempts to elicit false confessions from air force prisoners of war. *Bulletin of the New York Academy of Medicine* 1957; 33:616–626; quote on p. 617.

3. Amnesty International: *Report on Torture.* New York: Farrar, Straus & Giroux, 1973.

4. KUBARK Counterintelligence Manual (1963), p. 90. Quoted in F W Putnam: *The Way We Are: How States of Mind Influence Our Identities, Personality, and Potential for Change.* New York: IP Books, 2016, p. 373.

5. Former justice Alex Kozinsky of the Ninth Circuit Court of Appeals, as quoted in M C Nussbaum: *Citadels of Pride: Sexual Assault, Accountability, and Reconciliation.* New York: Norton, 2021, p. 143.

6. R Lloyd: *Girls Like Us: Fighting for a World Where Girls Are Not for Sale, an Activist Finds Her Calling and Heals Herself.* New York: HarperCollins, 2011, pp. 95–96.

7. K Richards & M Jagger: "Under My Thumb." In: *Aftermath.* London: Decca Records, 1966.

8. O Patterson: *Slavery and Social Death.* Cambridge, MA: Harvard University Press, 1982.

9. M Gessen: *Surviving Autocracy.* New York: Riverhead Books, 2020, p. 47.

10. Ibid., p. 111.

11. M Rothberg: *The Implicated Subject: Beyond Victims and Perpetrators.* Stanford, CA: Stanford University Press, 2019.

Chapter Two: The Rules of Equality

1. Quoted in K Young: "Our Freedom Is America's Freedom," *New York Times,* June 20, 2021, p. SR 5.

2. J Rawls: *A Theory of Justice.* Revised Edition. Cambridge, MA: Harvard University Press, 1999.

3. Quoted in L Weschler: *A Miracle, a Universe: Settling Accounts with Torturers.* New York: Pantheon, 1990, p. 244.

4. M C Nussbaum: *Citadels of Pride: Sexual Assault, Accountability, and Reconciliation.* New York: Norton, 2021, pp. 41–56.

5. S Jacoby: *Wild Justice: The Evolution of Revenge.* New York: Harper & Row, 1983.

6. Retrieved from "Revenge Is Sour," The Complete Works of George Orwell, http://www.george-orwell.org/Revenge_is_Sour/0.html.

7. J Murphy: "The Retributive Emotions." In: J G Murphy & J Hampton (Eds.): *Forgiveness and Mercy.* Cambridge, UK: Cambridge University Press, 1988, pp. 1–9.

8. R London: *Crime, Punishment, and Restorative Justice: From the Margins to the Mainstream.* Boulder, CO: First Forum Press, 2011, p. 64.

9. Ibid., pp. 74–75.

10. E Erikson: *Childhood and Society.* New York: Norton, 1950.

11. I am indebted for this observation, as for so much else, to the pioneering work of my mother, a psychoanalyst and researcher who studied the moral emotions. See H B Lewis: *Psychic War in Men and Women.* New York: New York University Press, 1976, pp. 71–72.

12. C Miller: *Know My Name: A Memoir.* New York: Viking, 2019, pp. 349–350.

13. E Erez: Who's afraid of the big bad victim? Victim impact statements as victim empowerment and enhancement of justice. *Criminal Law Review;* July 1999, 545–556.

14. B Williams: *Shame and Necessity.* Berkeley: University of California Press, 1990, p. 80.

Chapter Three: Patriarchy

1. C A MacKinnon: *Feminism Unmodified: Discourses on Life and Law.* Cambridge, MA: Harvard University Press, 1987, p. 169.

2. United Nations: *The World's Women 2015: Trends and Statistics.* Department of Economic and Social Affairs, Statistics Division, 2015.

3. P Tjaden & N Thoennes: *Prevalence, Incidence, and Consequences of Violence Against Women: Findings from the National Violence Against Women Survey.* US Department of Justice, National Institute of Justice, 1998. M J Breiding, S G Smith, K C Basile, et al.: Prevalence and characteristics of sexual violence, stalking, and intimate partner violence victimization: National Intimate Partner and Sexual Violence Survey. *Morbidity and Mortality Weekly Report, Surveillance Summaries* 2014; 63:1–18.

4. "Wartime Sexual Violence," Wikipedia, https://en.wikipedia.org/wiki/Wartime_sexual_violence#1974_to_1992.

5. J D Foubert, A Clark-Taylor & A F Wall: Is campus rape primarily a serial or one-time problem: Evidence from a multi-campus study. *Violence Against Women* 2019; 25:1–16.

6. "Prevention Strategies," CDC, www.cdc.gov/violenceprevention/child abuseandneglect/prevention.html.

7. J Herman, D Russell & K Trocki: Long-term effects of incestuous abuse in childhood. *American Journal of Psychiatry* 1986; 143:1293–1296.

8. J L Herman: *Father-Daughter Incest*. Cambridge, MA: Harvard University Press, 1981.

9. R Lanius: "Restoration of the Hijacked Self: Toward Embodiment and Connection." Lecture at 32nd Boston International Trauma Conference, May 27, 2021.

10. V Springora: *Consent* (English translation by R Lehrer). New York: HarperCollins, 2021, p. 156.

11. J G Noll: Child sexual abuse as a unique risk factor for the development of psychopathology: The compounded convergence of mechanisms. *Annual Review of Clinical Psychology* 2021; 17:1–26.

12. Ibid.

13. R Kluft: "On the Apparent Invisibility of Incest." In: R Kluft (Ed.): *Incest-Related Syndromes of Adult Psychopathology*. Washington, DC: American Psychiatric Association Press, 1990, p. 25.

14. A Dworkin: Prostitution and male supremacy. *Michigan Journal of Gender & Law* 1993; 1:1.

15. J G Noll, P K Trickett, W W Harris, et al.: The cumulative burden borne by offspring whose mothers were sexually abused as children: Descriptive results from a multigenerational study. *Journal of Interpersonal Violence* 2009; 24:424–449.

16. C S Widom, S J Czaja & K A DuMont: Intergenerational transmission of child abuse and neglect: Real or detection bias? *Science* 2015; 347:1480–1485. J Kaufman & E Zigler: Do abused children become abusive parents? *American Journal of Orthopsychiatry* 1987; 57:186–192.

17. United Nations: *Ending Violence Against Women: From Words to Action, Study of the Secretary-General (Overview)*. UN Women, 2006, p. iv.

18. C P Smith & F J Freyd: Institutional betrayal. *American Psychologist* 2014; 69:575–587.

19. K A Lonsway & J Archambault: The "justice gap" for sexual assault cases: Future directions for research and reform. *Violence Against Women* 2012; 18:145–168.

20. B R Hagerty: "An Epidemic of Disbelief: What New Research Reveals About Sexual Predators, and Why Police Fail to Catch Them," *The Atlantic,* August 2019.

21. M S Morabito, L M Williams & A Pattavina: *Decision Making in Sexual Assault Cases: Replication Research on Sexual Violence Case Attrition in the U.S.* Washington, DC: US Department of Justice, 2019.

22. J Manning: "Survivors Deserve Justice," *New York Times,* September 29, 2021, p. A20.

23. M Bowdler: *Is Rape a Crime? A Memoir, an Investigation, and a Manifesto.* New York: Flatiron Books, 2020, p. 145.

24. R Campbell, S R Wasco, C E Ahrens, et al.: Preventing the "second rape": Rape survivors' experiences with community service providers. *Journal of Interpersonal Violence* 2001; 16:1239–1259.

25. D Lisak, L Gardinier, A C Nicksa, et al.: False allegations of sexual assault: An analysis of ten years of reported cases. *Violence Against Women* 2010; 16:1318–1334.

26. S Gagnon & A Wagner: Acute stress and episodic memory retrieval: Neurobiological mechanisms and behavioral consequences. *Annals of the New York Academy of Sciences* 2016; 1369:55–75.

27. J L Herman: Crime and memory. *Bulletin of the American Academy of Psychiatry and Law* 1995; 23:5–17. D Brown, A W Scheflin & D C Hammond: *Memory, Trauma Treatment, and the Law.* New York: W W Norton & Company, 1998.

28. R McMahan: *Fortunate Daughter: A Memoir of Reconciliation.* Berkeley, CA: She Writes Press, 2021, pp. 106–107, 116–118.

29. M Alexander: *The New Jim Crow: Mass Incarceration in the Age of Colorblindness.* New York: New Press, 2010.

30. A S Simmons: *Love WITH Accountability: Digging Up the Roots of Child Sexual Abuse.* Chico, CA: AK Press, 2019.

Chapter Four: Acknowledgment

1. A Brodsky: *Sexual Justice: Supporting Victims, Ensuring Due Process, and Resisting the Conservative Backlash.* New York: Metropolitan Books, 2021, p. 76.

2. K Dwyer, D Walsh & A H Webb: *Call to Reform the Archdiocese of Boston.* Unpublished manuscript, 2003.

3. John Harvard's Journal: "Neither Comfort nor Cover: A Withering Investigation of Sexual Harassment," *Harvard Magazine,* May–June 2021, 22–23.

4. A Brodsky: personal communication, August 25, 2021.

Chapter Five: Apology

1. J Curran: "Sex Scandal Big Business for Lawyer," Associated Press, April 1, 2002.

2. A Lazare: *On Apology*. New York: Oxford University Press, 2004.

3. N Tavuchis: *Mea Culpa: A Sociology of Apology and Reconciliation*. Stanford, CA: Stanford University Press, 1991.

4. R McMahan: *Fortunate Daughter: A Memoir of Reconciliation*. Berkeley, CA: She Writes Press, 2021.

5. R McMahan: interview, June 3, 2021.

6. E Schatzow and J L Herman: Breaking secrecy: Adult survivors disclose to their families. *Psychiatric Clinics of North America* 1989; 12:337–350.

7. H Zehr: *Changing Lenses: A New Focus for Crime and Justice*. Scottsdale, PA: Herald Press, 1990.

8. D Konstan: *Before Forgiveness: The Origins of a Moral Idea*. New York: Cambridge University Press, 2010.

9. E Ensler: *The Apology*. New York: Bloomsbury, 2019.

10. V (E Ensler): "The Alchemy of Apology." Lecture at the 32nd Boston International Trauma Conference, May 29, 2021.

11. R Enright: *Forgiveness Is a Choice: A Step-by-Step Process for Resolving Anger and Restoring Hope*. Washington, DC: American Psychological Association, 2002.

12. A M Hunter: "The Thorny Question of Forgiveness." Sermon delivered at Maple Street United Methodist Church, Lynn, Massachusetts, October 17, 1999. Unpublished manuscript provided by author. Boston: Safe Havens Interfaith Partnership Against Domestic Violence, pp. 4–5.

13. D Martin: "Harm, Hope and Healing: International Dialogue on the Clergy Sex Abuse Scandal" Lecture at Marquette University Law School Conference, Milwaukee, Wisconsin, April 4, 2011.

14. Y Gorelik: "Exploring the Complexities of Forgiveness," *The Conversation*, January 26, 2017, https://theconversation.com/exploring-the-complexities-of-forgiveness-71774#.

Chapter Six: Accountability

1. J Brown: "Inaugural," *New York Times Magazine*, January 31, 2021, p. 27.

2. Alliance for Safety and Justice: *Crime Survivors Speak: National Survey of Victims' Views*. San Francisco, CA: David Binder Research, 2016.

3. D Paterson & R Campbell: Why rape survivors participate in the criminal justice system. *Journal of Community Psychology* 2010; 38:191–205.

4. J Braithwaite: "The Fundamentals of Restorative Justice." In: D Sullivan and L Tiffit (Eds.): *Handbook of Restorative Justice: A Global Perspective*: London: Routledge, 2006, pp. 35–43.

5. J Braithwaite: *Crime, Shame, and Reintegration*. Cambridge, UK: Cambridge University Press, 1989, p. 156.

6. Ibid.

7. J Stubbs: "Domestic Violence and Women's Safety: Feminist Challenges to Restorative Justice." In: H Strang & J Braithwaite (Eds.): *Restorative Justice and Family Violence*. Cambridge, UK: Cambridge University Press, 2002, pp. 42–61. K Daly: Restorative justice: The real story. *Punishment & Society* 2001; 4:55–79. A Smith: Preface. In: C-I Chen, J Dulani & L Lakshmi (Eds.): *The Revolution Starts at Home: Confronting Intimate Violence Within Activist Communities*. Chico, CA: AK Press, 2016, pp. xiii–xvii.

8. H Zehr: *Changing Lenses: A New Focus for Crime and Justice*. Scottsdale, PA: Herald Press, 1990, p. 172.

9. H Zehr: *Transcending: Reflections of Crime Victims*. Intercourse, PA: Good Books, 2001, p. 195.

10. P Gobodo-Madikizele: interview, October 12, 2009.

11. K Daly: "The Limits of Restorative Justice." In: D Sullivan & L Tifft (Eds.): *Handbook of Restorative Justice: A Global Perspective*. New York: Routledge, 2006, pp. 134–144.

12. The Chrysalis Collective: "Beautiful, Difficult, Powerful: Ending Sexual Assault Through Transformative Justice." In: C-I Chen, J Dulani & L L Piepzna-Samarasinha: *The Revolution Starts at Home: Confronting Intimate Violence Within Activist Communities*. Chico, CA: AK Press, 2016, pp. 189–206.

13. J Stubbs: "Domestic Violence and Women's Safety: Feminist Challenges to Restorative Justice." In: H Strang & J Braithwaite: *Restorative Justice and Family Violence*. Cambridge, UK: Cambridge University Press, 2002, pp. 43–61. D A Leidholdt: *Sanctuary for Families*. New York: Unpublished memorandum, November 2021.

14. G Duwe: Can circles of support and accountability (COSA) work in the United States: Preliminary results from a randomized experiment in Minnesota. *Sexual Abuse: A Journal of Research and Treatment* 2013; 25:143–165.

15. A Lanni: Taking restorative justice seriously. *Buffalo Law Review* 2021; 69:635–681.

16. R London: *Crime, Punishment, and Restorative Justice: From the Margins to the Mainstream*. Boulder, CO: First Forum Press, 2011, p. 177.

17. Ibid., p. 183.

18. M Kaba: *We Do This 'Til We Free Us: Abolitionist Organizing and Transformative Justice*. Chicago, IL: Haymarket Books, 2021.

19. B Naylor: Effective justice for victims of sexual assault: Taking up the debate on alternative pathways. *UNSW Law Journal* 2010; 33:662–684.

20. BishopAccountability.org: https://www.bishopaccountability.org.

21. K Dwyer: personal communication, November 2020.

22. *Fleites et al. v. MindGeek et al.*, US District Court, Central District of California, Case No. 2:21-cv-4920, filed June 17, 2021.

23. M Farley: personal communication, September 25, 2021. I am also indebted to Laila Mickelwait, founder and CEO of the Justice Defense Fund, for an update on the status of these cases, June 19, 2022. For additional information, see S Kolhatkar: "The Perils of Pornhub," *New Yorker*, June 20, 2022, pp. 30–39.

Chapter Seven: Restitution

1. A M Jones: "Reparations Now, Reparations Tomorrow, Reparations Forever." In: *Reparations Now!* Spartanburg, SC: Hub City Press, 2021.

2. S Herman & M Waul: *Repairing the Harm: A New Vision for Crime Victim Compensation in America*. Washington, DC: National Center for Victims of Crime, 2004, p. 57.

3. I Cho & A Kim: "Lawsuit Alleges Harvard Ignored Sexual Harassment Complaints Against John Comaroff for Years," *Harvard Crimson*, February 9, 2022.

4. "Guide for a Trauma-Informed Law Enforcement Initiative," City of Cambridge, 2020, https://www.cambridgema.gov/-/media/Files/policedepartment/SpecialReports/guideforatraumainformedlawenforcementinitiative.pdf.

5. B Hamm, PsyD: personal communication, 2020.

6. F Camacho: Sexually exploited youth: A view from the bench. *Touro Law Review* 2015; 31:377–382.

7. Ibid., p. 379.

8. F Camacho: interview, November 8, 2021.

9. F Camacho: "Human Trafficking and the Courts—the Evolution of Perceptions and the Responses to Prostitution and Human Trafficking over the Last Thirty-Five Years." Lecture at Sanctuary for Families Conference, October 1, 2019.

10. S Wang-Breal: *Blowin' Up*. Documentary film. New York: Once in a Blue Films, 2019.

11. H, J & P: "Dear Johns—An Open Letter to Sex Buyers," *Boston Globe*, March 18, 2019, p. A9.

12. T Serita: interview, December 30, 2021.

13. See, for example, "Sex, Carceralism, and Capitalism." In: A Srinivasan: *The Right to Sex: Feminism in the Twenty-First Century*. New York: Farrar, Straus & Giroux, 2021, pp. 149–179.

14. L Platt, P Grenfell, R Meiksin, et al.: Associations between sex work laws and sex workers' health. *PLoS Med* 2018; 15(12):e1002680.

15. R Moran & M Farley: Consent, coercion, and culpability: Is prostitution stigmatized work or an exploitative and violent practice rooted in sex, race and class inequality? *Archives of Sexual Behavior* 2018; 48:1947–1953. M Farley: Making the connections: Resource extraction, prostitution, poverty, climate change, and human rights. *International Journal of Human Rights* 2021; https://www.tandfonline.com/doi/full/10.1080/13642987.2021.1997999.

16. New Zealand Prostitution Law Review Committee: *Report of the Prostitution Law Review Committee on the Operation of the Prostitution Reform Act of 2003*. Wellington, New Zealand, 2008.

17. W Kaime-Atterhog: *Perspectives on the Swedish Model to Prevent and Combat Prostitution and Trafficking for Purposes of Sexual Exploitation*. Stockholm: House of Plenty Foundation, 2021.

18. M Waltman: *Pornography: The Politics of Legal Challenges*. New York: Oxford University Press, 2021. See in particular Chapter 9: "Substantive Equality Prostitution Law, 1999–2019," pp. 334–370, for a comprehensive review of the evidence, including the substantial literature published in Swedish as well as English.

19. F Camacho: interview, November 8, 2021.

20. F Camacho: "Human Trafficking and the Courts—The Evolution of Perceptions and the Responses to Prostitution and Human Trafficking over the Last Thirty-Five Years." Lecture at Sanctuary for Families "Vision for Change" Conference, New York, October 27, 2019.

21. F Camacho: interview, November 8, 2021.

Chapter Eight: Rehabilitation

1. Quoted in A R Ackerman & J S Levenson: *Healing from Sexual Violence: The Case for Vicarious Restorative Justice*. Brandon, VT: Safer Society Press, 2019, p. 89.

2. M DeLisi, A E Kosloski, M G Vaughn, et al.: Does childhood sexual abuse victimization translate into juvenile sexual offending? New evidence. *Violence and Victims* 2014; 29:620–635.

3. D Dehart & S Lynch: *Women's and Girls' Pathways Through the Criminal Legal System: Addressing Trauma, Mental Health, and Marginalization*. San Diego, CA: Cognella, 2021.

4. G Duwe: Can circles of support and accountability (COSA) work in the United States: Preliminary results from a randomized experiment in Minnesota. *Sexual Abuse: A Journal of Research and Treatment* 2013; 25:143–165.

5. J L Herman: Considering sex offenders: A model of addiction. *Signs: Journal of Women in Culture and Society* 1988; 13:695–724.

6. R L Snyder: *No Visible Bruises: What We Don't Know About Domestic Violence Can Kill Us.* New York: Bloomsbury, 2019.

7. D Rosenfeld: "Who Are You Calling a 'Ho'? Challenging the Porn Culture on Campus." In: M T Reist & A Bray (Eds.): *Big Porn Inc: Exposing the Harms of the Pornography Industry.* Victoria, Australia: Spinifex Press, 2011, pp. 41–52; quote on p. 45.

8. H M Zinzow & M Thompson: A longitudinal study of risk factors for repeated sexual coercion and assault in U.S. college men. *Archives of Sexual Behavior* 2015; 44:213–222. J D Foubert, A Clark-Taylor & A F Wall: Is campus rape primarily a serial or one-time problem? Evidence from a multi-campus study. *Violence Against Women* 2019; 25:1–16.

9. "About Us," Domestic Abuse Intervention Programs, https://www.the duluthmodel.org/about-us.

10. R E Dobash, R P Dobash, K Cavanaugh, et al.: *Changing Violent Men.* Thousand Oaks, CA: Sage, 2000. E Gondolf: *Batterer Intervention Systems: Issues, Outcomes, and Recommendations.* Thousand Oaks, CA: Sage Publications, 2002.

11. E Gondolf: *The Future of Batterer Programs: Reassessing Evidence-Based Practice.* Boston, MA: Northeastern University Press, 2012.

12. U Douglas, D Bathrick & P A Perry: Deconstructing male violence against women: The Men Stopping Violence community-accountability model. *Violence Against Women* 2008; 14:247–261.

13. J D Stinson & J V Becker: *Treating Sex Offenders: An Evidence-Based Manual.* New York: Guilford, 2013.

14. M Koss: The RESTORE Program of Restorative Justice for sex crimes: Vision, process, and outcomes. *Journal of Interpersonal Violence* 2014; 29:1623–1660.

15. A R Ackerman & J S Levenson: *Healing from Sexual Violence: The Case for Vicarious Restorative Justice.* Brandon, VT: Safer Society Press, 2019.

Chapter Nine: Prevention

1. S Abdulali: *What We Talk About When We Talk About Rape.* New York: New Press, 2018, p. 133.

2. K M Boyle: Social psychological processes that facilitate sexual assault with the fraternity party subculture. *Sociology Compass* 2015; 9:386–399. K McCray:

Intercollegiate athletics and sexual violence: A review of literature and recommendations for future study. *Trauma, Violence and Abuse* 2015; 16:438–443.

3. P R Sanday: *Fraternity Gang Rape: Sex, Brotherhood, and Privilege on Campus.* New York: New York University Press, 2007.

4. F W Putnam: *Something Terrible Happened to These Children: Memoir of a Child Abuse Doctor.* Unpublished manuscript, 2022.

5. D Rosenfeld: Uncomfortable conversations: Confronting the reality of target rape on campus. *Harvard Law Review Forum* 2015; 128:359–380.

6. J D Foubert, A Clark-Taylor & A F Wall: Is campus rape primarily a serial or one-time problem: Evidence from a multi-campus study. *Violence Against Women* 2019; 25:1–16.

7. MASOC Campus Sexual Misconduct Conference, William James College, Boston, Massachusetts, June 10, 2021.

8. J S Santelli, S A Grilo, T-H Choo, et al.: Does sex education before college protect students from sexual assault in college? *PLoS ONE* 2018; 13(11):e0205951.

9. P Orenstein: "Ignoring Pornography Won't Make It Go Away," *New York Times,* June 15, 2021.

10. C A MacKinnon: *Feminism Unmodified: Discourses on Life and Law.* Cambridge, MA: Harvard University Press, 1987, p. 171.

11. S D Hill: interviews, November 18, 2020, and December 10, 2020.

12. K Peterson, P Sharps, V Banyard, et al.: An evaluation of two dating violence prevention programs on a college campus. *Journal of Interpersonal Violence Online* 2016; 1–26. https://doi,org/10.1177/088626051663069. K Alegria-Flores, K Raker, R K Pleasants, et al.: Preventing interpersonal violence on college campuses: The effect of One Act training on bystander intervention. *Journal of Interpersonal Violence* 2017; 32:1103–1126.

13. A L Coker, B S Fisher, H M Bush, et al.: Evaluation of the Green Dot Bystander Intervention to reduce interpersonal violence among college students across three campuses. *Violence Against Women* 2015; 21:1507–1527.

14. T N Richards: An updated review of institutions of higher education's responses to sexual assault: Results from a nationally representative sample. *Journal of Interpersonal Violence* 2019; 34:1983–2012.

15. C Mengo & B M Black: Violence victimization on a college campus: Impact on GPA and school dropout. *Journal of College Student Retention: Research, Theory & Practice* 2015; 16:1–15.

16. Anonymous: "Dear Harvard: You Win," *Harvard Crimson,* March 31, 2014.

17. John Harvard's Journal: "Harvard's Sexual Assault Problem," *Harvard Magazine,* November–December 2015, 18–20.

18. K J Holland, L M Cortina & J J Freyd: Compelled disclosure of college sexual assault. *American Psychologist* 2018; 73:256–268.

19. J F Isselbacher and A Y Su: "With End of Sanctions, Khurana Bids Signature Policy Proposal Goodbye," *Harvard Crimson*, July 1, 2020.

20. S C Chu & I M Lewis: "Prevalence of Sexual Misconduct at Harvard Remains Unchanged from Four Years Ago, AAU Survey Finds," *Harvard Crimson*, October 15, 2019.

21. J F Isselbacher and A Y Su: "With End of Sanctions, Khurana Bids Signature Policy Proposal Goodbye," *Harvard Crimson*, July 1, 2020.

22. A Brodsky: *Sexual Justice: Supporting Victims, Ensuring Due Process, and Resisting the Conservative Backlash.* New York: Metropolitan Books, 2021.

23. L Ferre-Sadurni: "He Is Accused of Rape but Has 'a Good Family,'" *New York Times*, July 3, 2019, p. 1.

24. "Federal Judge Vacates Part of Trump Administration's Title IX Sexual Harassment Rule," National Women's Law Center, August 11, 2021, https:// nwlc.org/resources/federal-judge-vacates-part-of-trump-administrations-title -ix-sexual-harassment.

25. R Frost: interview, September 3, 2020.

26. MASOC Campus Sexual Misconduct Conference, William James College, Boston, Massachusetts, June 10, 2021.

27. D R Karp: *The Little Book of Restorative Justice for Colleges and Universities.* New York: Good Books, 2015.

28. D R Karp: "Restorative Justice and Responsive Regulation in Higher Education: The Complex Web of Campus Sexual Assault Policy in the United States, and a Restorative Alternative." In: G Burford, V Braithwaite & J Braithwaite (Eds.): *Restorative and Responsive Human Services.* New York: Routledge, 2019, pp. 143–164.

29. M Orcutt, P M Petrowski, D R Karp, et al.: Restorative Justice approaches to the informal resolution of student sexual misconduct. *Journal of College and University Law* 2020; 45.

Conclusion: *The Longest Revolution*

1. A Hill: *Believing.* New York: Viking, 2021.

2. J Mitchell: Women: The longest revolution. *New Left Review* 1966; 40.

3. United Nations General Assembly: "Convention on the Elimination of All Forms of Discrimination Against Women," UN Human Rights Office of the High Commissioner, December 18, 1979, https://www.ohchr.org/en /professionalinterest/pages/cedaw.aspx.

4. "15 Years of the United Nations Special Rapporteur on Violence Against Women, Its Causes and Consequences (1994–2009)—A Critical Review," UN Human Rights Office of the High Commissioner, https://www.ohchr.org /Documents/Issues/Women/15YearReviewofVAWMandate.pdf.

5. "Violence Against Women, Its Causes and Consequences: Report of the Special Rapporteur on Violence Against Women, Its Causes and Consequences," United Nations, https://undocs.org/A/HRC/41/42.

6. www.dol.gov/agencies/wb/data/facts.

7. N Gartrell, J L Herman, S Olarte, et al.: Psychiatrist-patient sexual contact: Results of a national survey, I: Prevalence. *American Journal of Psychiatry* 1986; 143:1126–1131.

8. Office for Diversity, Equity, and Inclusion: https://diversity.defense.gov.

9. C A MacKinnon: "#MeToo Has Done What the Law Could Not," *New York Times*, February 4, 2018.

10. M Fisher: "As Abortion Rights Expand, US Joins the Telling Exceptions," *New York Times*, September 10, 2021, p. A6.

11. T Burke & M Ramirez: "We Cannot End Racism Without Listening to Sexual Violence Survivors," *ELLE*, July 7, 2020.

12. M Farley, A Cotton, J Lynne, et al.: Prostitution and trafficking in nine countries: Update on violence and post traumatic stress disorder. *Journal of Trauma Practice* 2003; 2:33–74. M Farley: "Prostitution: An Extreme Form of Girls' Sexualization." In: EL Zurbriggen & T-A Roberts (Eds.): *The Sexualization of Girls and Girlhood*. New York: Oxford University Press, 2013, pp. 166–194.

13. M Waltman: *Pornography: The Politics of Legal Challenges*. New York: Oxford University Press, 2021.

Acknowledgments

1. J L Herman: Helen Block Lewis: A memoir of three generations. *Psychoanalytic Psychology* 2013; 30:528–534.

INDEX

Judith L. Herman, MD, is a professor of psychiatry at Harvard Medical School. Herman is also the cofounder of the Victims of Violence Program, which for thirty-eight years provided trauma treatment, professional training, and victim advocacy in a public hospital. She is a recipient of the Lifetime Achievement Award from the International Society for Traumatic Stress Studies and is a distinguished life fellow of the American Psychiatric Association.